IN JESUS YOU ARE...

WHEN WOMEN ARE
EQUIPPED WITH THE
KNOWLEDGE OF GOD'S
TRUTH, THE WORLD
IS TRANSFORMED ONE
WOMAN AT A TIME.

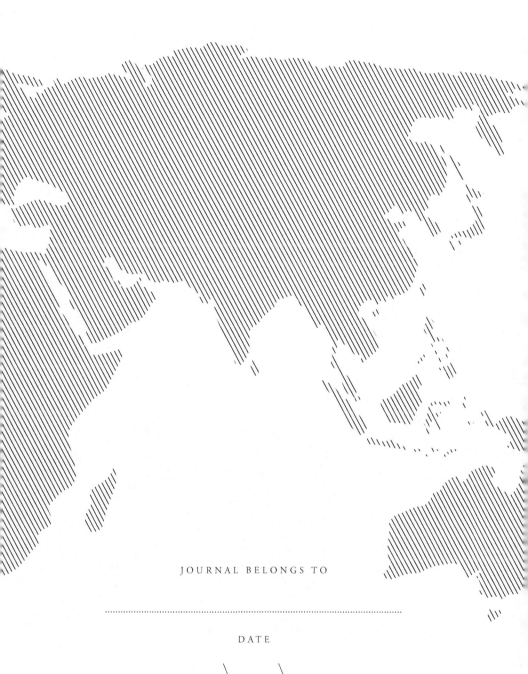

JOURNAL BELONGS TO

....

DATE

\   \

....

CONTENTS

You

HAVE BEEN
PRAYED FOR;
IT IS NOT A
COINCIDENCE
YOU ARE
PARTICIPATING
IN THIS
STUDY.

WELCOME FRIEND!

We are glad you have decided to join us in this Bible study! You have been prayed for; it is not a coincidence you are participating in this study.

Our prayer for you is simple: that you will grow closer to our Lord as you dig into His Word each and every day. Each day before you read the assigned passage, pray and ask God to help you understand it. Invite Him to speak to you through His Word. Then listen. Believe He will be faithful to speak to you, and be faithful to listen and obey.

Take time to read the verses over and over again. The Bible tells us that if we seek wisdom like silver, and search for it like hidden treasure, then we will understand how to fear the Lord, and we will discover knowledge about God (Prov 2:4-5).

All of us here at Love God Greatly can't wait for you to get started, and we hope to see you at the finish line. Endure, persevere, press on; don't give up! Finish well what you are beginning today.

We will be here every step of the way, cheering for you! We are in this together. Be expectant that God has much in store for you in this study. Journey with us as we learn to love God greatly with our lives!

WE NEED EACH
OTHER, AND WE
LIVE LIFE BETTER
TOGETHER. WOULD
YOU CONSIDER
REACHING OUT AND
DOING THIS STUDY
WITH SOMEONE?

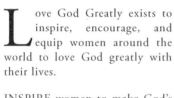

Love God Greatly exists to inspire, encourage, and equip women around the world to love God greatly with their lives.

INSPIRE women to make God's Word a priority in their daily lives through Bible study resources.

ENCOURAGE women in their walks with God through online community and personal accountability.

EQUIP women to grow in their faith so they can effectively reach others for Christ.

We start with a simple Bible reading plan, but it doesn't stop there. Some women gather in homes and churches locally, while others connect online with women across the globe, Whatever the method, we lovingly lock arms and unite for this purpose: to love God greatly with our lives.

At Love God Greatly, you'll find real, authentic women. You'll find women who desire less of each other, and a whole lot more of Jesus. Women who long to know God through His Word because we believe that truth transforms and sets us free. Women who are better together, saturated in God's Word and in community with one another.

Love God Greatly is committed to providing quality Bible study materials and believes finances should never get in the way of a woman being able to participate in one of our studies. All journals are available to download for free from LoveGodGreatly.com.

Our journals and books are also available for sale on Amazon. Search for "Love God Greatly" to see all of our Bible study journals and books.

YOU'LL FIND WOMEN WHO ARE IMPERFECT, YET FORGIVEN.

Love God Greatly is a 501 (C) (3) non-profit organization. Funding for Love God Greatly comes through donations and proceeds from our online Bible study journals and books.

One-hundred percent of proceeds go directly back into supporting Love God Greatly and helping us inspire, encourage, and equip women all over the world with God's Word.

Arm-in-arm and hand-in-hand, let's do this together.

OUR MISSION

THE NEED

Billions of women around the world don't have access to God's Word in their native language. Those who do, don't have access to women's Bible studies designed and written with them in mind.

THE MISSION

At Love God Greatly, we create Bible studies in 35+ languages. We equip missionaries, ministries, local churches, and women with God's Word at an unprecedented rate by allowing our journals to be downloaded from our international sites at no cost.

Through studying the Bible in their own language with like-minded communities, women are trained and equipped with God's Word.

We believe when women read and apply God's Word to their lives and embrace His unchanging love for them, the world is a better place. We know one woman in God's Word can change a family, a community, and a nation... one woman at a time.

PARTNER WITH US

We would love for you to join us in our mission of giving women all over the world access to God's Word and quality Bible study resources! For any questions or for more information, email us or visit us online. We would love to hear from you!

INFO@LOVEGODGREATLY.COM

LOVEGODGREATLY.COM

AT LOVE GOD GREATLY,
WE CREATE BIBLE STUDIES
IN 35+ LANGUAGES.

SOAP

Bible Study Method

A t Love God Greatly, we believe that the Word of God is living and active. The words of Scripture are powerful and effective and relevant for life in all times and all cultures. In order to interpret the Bible correctly, we need an understanding of the context and culture of the original writings.

As we study the Bible, we use the SOAP Bible Study Method. The acronym stands for Scripture, Observation, Application, and Prayer. It's one thing simply to read Scripture. When you interact with it, intentionally slowing down to reflect, truths start jumping off the page. The SOAP Method allows us to dig deeper into Scripture and see more than we would if we simply read the verses. It allows us not only to be hearers of the Word, but doers as well (Jas 1:22).

YOU WILL NEVER WASTE TIME IN GOD'S WORD. IT IS LIVING, POWERFUL, AND EFFECTIVE, AND HE SPEAKS TO US THROUGH IT.

In this journal, we read a passage of Scripture and then apply the SOAP Method to specific verses. Using this method allows us to glean a greater understanding of Scripture, which allows us to apply it effectively to our lives.

The most important ingredients in the SOAP Method are your interaction with God's Word and your application of it to your life. Take time to study it carefully, discovering the truth of God's character and heart for the world.

"I AM"

...d who made the world
...thing in it, who is Lord
...es and earth, does not
... Temples made by human
... nor is he served by human
..., as it he needed anything,
... he himself gives life and
... and anything to everyone.

→ He is eternal
★ - God is not made or created
- He is eternal, always, everlasting
- Lifegiver
- Creator of all
- He is everywhere
- He cannot be co...
- True God

★ Ruler my...
- own my...
- He created me
★ Keep my heart/worship on Him a...
- Remember everything is created by
Him + for Him.

Dear Lord,
Thank you for loving me
beyond my understanding.
Thank you for giving me life and
family. Help my heart to it's
focus on you and not on my
selfish desires. Forgive me when
I bring you down to my human
understanding. You are the Ruler o...
...ing of all!
Amen

SOAP
Bible Study Method

S

STANDS FOR SCRIPTURE

Physically write out the SOAP verses.

You'll be amazed at what God will reveal to you just by taking the time to slow down and write out what you are reading!

SOAP

WEEK 1 • MONDAY

SCRIPTURE / *Write out the SOAP verses*

Then I heard a loud voice in heaven saying, "The salvation and the power and the kingdom of our God, and the (ruling authority) of his Christ, have now come, because the accuser of our brothers and sisters, the one who accuses them (day and night) before our God, has been thrown down. Revelation 12:10

But the Lord is faithful, and he will strengthen you and protect you from the (evil one.) 2 Thessalonians 3:3

O

STANDS FOR OBSERVATION

What do you see in the verses that you're reading?

Who is the intended audience? Is there a repetition of words?

What words stand out to you?

OBSERVATION / *Write 3 - 4 observations*

Loud voice, powerful, all knowing
We are accused day and night, constant struggle
The Lord will help, establish and guard me
He's always there
He's is constant, a protector in my life, guardian

A •

STANDS FOR
APPLICATION

*This is when God's Word
becomes personal.*

*What is God saying to
you today? How can you
apply what you just read
to your own personal life?*

*What changes do you
need to make? Is there
action you need to take?*

APPLICATION / *Write down 1 - 2 applications*

Remind myself of God's strength is more powerful than anything
Memorize these verses and say them daily this week
Ask God to strengthen my faith in Him
Trust God that he will deliver me from evil
Pray for my brothers and sister's in Christ

PRAYER / *Write out a prayer over what you learned*

Dear Lord,

Thank you for being constant, faithful, and loving towards me
and my life. Help me to further my trust and faith in you
daily and through difficult times.

Help me to know you're alway there by my side, guarding,
and protecting me. Remind me of the suffering of others and
to be able to help and encourage them in their growth.

I ask all these things in Jesus name.
Amen

P •

STANDS FOR PRAYER

*Pray God's Word back to Him.
Spend time thanking Him.*

*If He has revealed something to you during
this time in His Word, pray about it.*

*If He has revealed some sin that is in your life, confess.
And remember, He loves you dearly.*

Do you remember singing the old hymns at church as a child? For me, that brings back memories full of both giggles and frowning. What do all these words of old mean? One song that puzzled me was '*On Christ, the solid Rock, I stand.*' What does it mean to stand on a solid rock that is no rock made of stone? I had no clue.

Through studying God's Word, I grew to understand that standing on a rock is about my foundation. My solid ground is the ground on which I stand to be a steadfast person. Through studying the Bible, I learned so much about my identity in Christ. I am not defined by what the world says I am, I'm not what I can achieve; I'm who Christ says I am. Through His Word, He tells me I'm loved. He tells me I'm a new creation. He tells me I'm made in His image.

> *WHEN MY HEART IS OVERWHELMED, I WANT TO GO TO THE ROCK THAT IS HIGHER THAN I.*

Four years ago I started translating for Love God Greatly. I was blessed so much by reading the words in English, thinking about how to translate them best and rereading my translation to make it better. I would consider all the words carefully. Fixing my eyes on Jesus while writing helped me to be aware of my Rock. The *Draw Near* study helped me to study God's Word in depth. The *Words Matter* study taught me so much about capturing thoughts and filling my mind with God's Truth. *Jesus Our Everything* taught me so much about the superiority of Christ. There is a lifetime of learning to be found in studying the Bible.

The Bible taught me so much about who God is. Through His Word, God teaches me how to stand on my Rock. When my heart is overwhelmed, I want to go to the Rock that is higher than I. For God is my refuge and my strong tower. More words of old, from songs of old. They don't make me giggle or frown anymore, now they fill my heart with awe and gratitude for who He is.

Willemien
LGG Dutch Branch

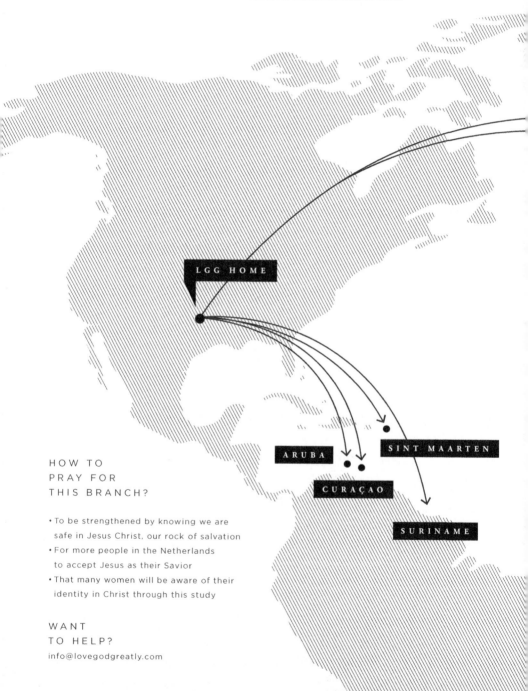

LANGUAGE
Dutch

GLOBAL
SPEAKERS
15,489,000

TO CONNECT WITH THIS BRANCH
Facebook: facebook.com/lggnl
Instagram: @lovegodgreatlynederlands
Email: lovegodgreatlynederlands@gmail.com
Website: lovegodgreatly.com/dutch

LGG HOME

ARUBA

SINT MAARTEN

CURAÇAO

SURINAME

HOW TO
PRAY FOR
THIS BRANCH?

• To be strengthened by knowing we are
  safe in Jesus Christ, our rock of salvation
• For more people in the Netherlands
  to accept Jesus as their Savior
• That many women will be aware of their
  identity in Christ through this study

WANT
TO HELP?
info@lovegodgreatly.com

THE NETHERLANDS

BELGIUM

Do you know someone
who could use our Love
God Greatly Bible studies
in the Dutch language?

If so, make sure to tell
them all the amazing
Bible study resources we
provide to help equip
them with God's Word!

Hutspot

INGREDIENTS

2¼ LB. FLOURY POTATOES

1½ LB CARROTS

ABOUT 4 LARGE ONIONS

2 TBSP OF BUTTER

SPLASH OF MILK

PEPPER AND SALT TO TASTE

DIRECTIONS

Peel the potatoes and chop them into chunks. Peel the carrots, and chop them into slices or small chunks. Peel the onions and chop them. Add all of this to a large pan with the boiling water along with some salt. Cook until the potatoes are done, about 20 minutes.

Use a potato masher to mash the potatoes, carrots, and onions. Season with pepper and salt. Add butter and milk until you've reached a smooth mash. Serve with a rookworst (Dutch smoked sausage), some meatballs, or top with cashews.

Eet smakelijk! (Enjoy)

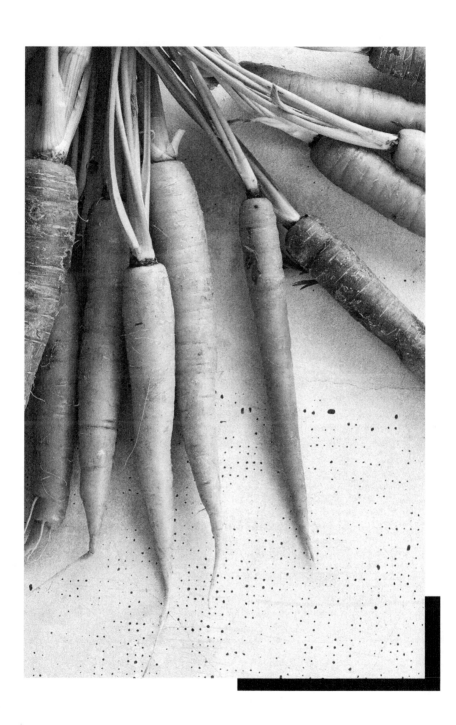

KNOW THESE TRUTHS

GOD LOVES YOU

God's Word says, "For this is the way God loved the world: He gave his one and only Son, so that everyone who believes in him will not perish but have eternal life" (John 3:16).

OUR SIN SEPARATES US FROM GOD

We are all sinners by nature and by choice, and because of this we are separated from God, who is holy. God's Word says, "for all have sinned and fall short of the glory of God" (Rom 3:23).

JESUS DIED SO YOU MIGHT HAVE LIFE

The consequence of sin is death, but God's free gift of salvation is available to us. Jesus took the penalty for our sin when He died on the cross.

God's Word says, "For the payoff of sin is death, but the gift of God is eternal life in Christ Jesus our Lord" (Rom 6:23); "But God demonstrates his own love for us, in that while we were still sinners, Christ died for us" (Rom 5:8).

JESUS LIVES!

Death could not hold Him, and three days after His body was placed in the tomb Jesus rose again, defeating sin and death forever. He lives today in heaven and is preparing a place in eternity for all who believe in Him.

Jesus says, "There are many dwelling places in my Father's house. Otherwise, I would have told you, because I am going away to make ready a place for you. And if I go and make ready a place for you, I will come again and take you to be with me, so that where I am you may be too" (John 14:2–3).

KNOW YOU CAN BE FORGIVEN

Accepting Jesus as your Savior is not about what you can do, but rather about having faith in what Jesus has already done. It takes recognizing that you are a sinner, believing that Jesus died for your sins, and asking for forgiveness by placing your full trust in Jesus' work on the cross on your behalf.

God's Word says, "if you confess with your mouth that Jesus is Lord and believe in your heart that God raised him from the dead, you will be saved. For with the heart one believes and thus has righteousness and with the mouth one confesses and thus has salvation" (Rom 10:9–10).

ACCEPT CHRIST'S FREE GIFT OF SALVATION

Practically, what does that look like? With a sincere heart, you can pray a simple prayer like this:

Jesus,
I know that I am a sinner. I don't want to live another day without embracing the love and forgiveness that You have for me. I ask for Your forgiveness. I believe that You died for my sins and rose from the dead. I surrender all that I am and ask You to be Lord of my life. Help me to turn from my sin and follow You. Teach me what it means to walk in freedom as I live under Your grace, and help me to grow in Your ways as I seek to know You more. Amen.

CONNECT AND GROW

If you just prayed this prayer (or something similar in your own words) we'd love to connect with you!

You can email us at info@lovegodgreatly.com. We'd love to celebrate with you, pray with you, and help you connect to a local church. We are here to encourage you as you begin your new life as a child of God.

Let's Begin

IN JESUS YOU ARE

Understanding Your Identity in Christ

Introduction

Identity is defined as who or what a person or thing is. It is easy to define our identity by our family, our career, our friends, our hobbies, or our nationality. We often determine our identity by our actions, our words, or our reputation (both perceived and real). We create an identity both consciously and subconsciously. We all have a distinct identity, but it can be hard to pinpoint how our identity was formed or how we've come to define ourselves the way we do. It can be hard to know if our identity is true, or if we have given ourselves a false identity.

WITHOUT KNOWING OUR TRUE IDENTITY, WE CANNOT LIVE IN THE WAY WE WERE DESIGNED TO LIVE.

Without knowing our true identity, we cannot live in the way we were designed to live. In Christ, we have a secure, unchanging identity. He has marked our lives by His life, death, and resurrection. His work on the cross has changed us, marking us as His own.

The sacrifice of Christ allows us to be made new. He has paid the penalty for our sins, allowing us to live without guilt or shame. He has covered our sin, making us a new creation. We are forgiven in Him, made righteous by His sacrifice. We are delivered from our former life, sealed as His for eternity.

Though it is often what we most struggle to believe, our identity in Christ remains fixed. He has chosen us. He has redeemed us. And He will never leave us. If we have chosen to place our faith in Christ we are God's children and we are forever secure in Him.

As you study your identity in Christ, ask God to continually reveal His love for you. Ask Him to uncover areas of your life where it is hard for you to believe His truth. God longs for you to know who you are in Him. Let's, together, search His Word for the truth of who we are in Jesus.

WEEK 1

○ *Monday – I Am A New Creation*
Read: 2 Corinthians 5:17; Colossians 3:9–10
SOAP: 2 Corinthians 5:17

○ *Tuesday – I Am Forgiven*
Read: Ephesians 1:7–8; 1 John 1:9
SOAP: Ephesians 1:7

○ *Wednesday – I Am Righteous*
Read: Romans 5:1–2
SOAP: Romans 5:1–2

○ *Thursday – I Am Delivered*
Read: Psalm 107:1–3; Isaiah 43:1–3; Romans 8:1–4
SOAP: Isaiah 43:1

○ *Friday – I Am Sealed*
Read: 2 Corinthians 1:21–22
SOAP: 2 Corinthians 1:21–22

WEEK 2

○ *Monday – I Am Rescued*
Read: John 3:16–17; Colossians 1:11–14; Hebrews 2:14–15
SOAP: Colossians 1:13

○ *Tuesday – I Am Saved*
Read: Romans 5:8–10; Ephesians 2:1–5
SOAP: Ephesians 2:4–5

○ *Wednesday – I Am Free*
Read: John 8:36; 2 Corinthians 3:17
SOAP: John 8:36

○ *Thursday – I Am Loved*
Read: 1 John 4:10–19; Romans 8:35–39
SOAP: 1 John 4:10

○ *Friday – I Am Received*
Read: Romans 15:7–9
SOAP: Romans 15:7

WEEK 3

- ○ *Monday – I Am Adopted*
  Read: Ephesians 1:5–6; Colossians 1:12–13
  SOAP: Ephesians 1:5

- ○ *Tuesday – I Am A Child of God*
  Read: John 1:12; 1 John 3:1–2
  SOAP: John 1:12

- ○ *Wednesday – I Am Chosen*
  Read: Ephesians 1:4; 1 Peter 2:9
  SOAP: 1 Peter 2:9

- ○ *Thursday – I Am A Citizen of Heaven*
  Read: Ephesians 2:19; Philippians 3:20
  SOAP: Philippians 3:20

- ○ *Friday – I Am Known by God*
  Read: Psalm 139:1–3; 1 Corinthians 8:3
  SOAP: Psalm 139:1

WEEK 4

- ○ *Monday – I Am Intentionally Made*
  Read: Psalm 139:13–18
  SOAP: Psalm 139:13–14

- ○ *Tuesday – I Am Blessed*
  Read: Numbers 6:24–26; 2 Corinthians 9:8–10; Ephesians 1:3
  SOAP: Ephesians 1:3

- ○ *Wednesday – I Am Equipped*
  Read: Ephesians 2:10; 2 Timothy 3:16–17
  SOAP: Ephesians 2:10

- ○ *Thursday – I Am Empowered*
  Read: 1 Corinthians 12:4–11; 2 Corinthians 12:9; Philippians 4:13
  SOAP: Philippians 4:13

- ○ *Friday – I Am A Conqueror*
  Read: 1 John 4:4
  SOAP: 1 John 4:4

YOUR GOALS

Write three goals you would like to focus on as you begin each day and dig into God's Word. Make sure you refer back to these goals throughout the next weeks to help you stay focused. You can do it!

ONE

....
....
....
....
....
....
....

TWO

....
....
....
....
....
....
....

THREE

....
....
....
....
....
....
....

So then, if anyone is in Christ, he is a new creation; what is old has passed away— look, what is new has come!

2 Corinthians 5:17

PRAY

*Write down your prayer requests
and praises for this week.*

....

....

....

....

....

....

....

....

....

....

....

....

WEEKLY CHALLENGE

*In Christ, you are a new creation! This week, record all the ways you have seen God
renew your life and make you a new creation in Christ. Ask God to reveal His work
in you as you seek Him this week.*

....

....

....

....

....

....

....

READ

2 Corinthians 5:17

So then, if anyone is in Christ, he is a new creation; what is old has passed away—look, what is new has come!

Colossians 3:9–10

Do not lie to one another since you have put off the old man with its practices 10 and have been clothed with the new man that is being renewed in knowledge according to the image of the one who created it.

SOAP / *2 Corinthians 5:17*
SCRIPTURE / *Write out the SOAP verses*

_____

_____

_____

_____

_____

_____

_____

_____

_____

_____

_____

_____

_____

_____

_____

_____

_____

_____

OBSERVATION / *Write 3 - 4 observations*

_____

_____

_____

_____

_____

_____

_____

_____

APPLICATION / *Write down 1 - 2 applications*

_____

_____

_____

_____

_____

_____

_____

_____

_____

_____

_____

PRAYER / *Write out a prayer over what you learned*

_____

_____

_____

_____

_____

_____

_____

_____

_____

_____

_____

_____

_____

_____

_____

SOAP

2 Corinthians 5:17

"So then, if anyone is in Christ, he is a new creation; what is old has passed away—look, what is new has come!"

INTO THE TEXT

Who do you think you are? Said with a certain attitude, it's a question that makes us feel defensive, out of place, or in the wrong. Asked with genuine interest, it can invite us to pause and reflect, considering all of the elements that make us who we are. Our ancestors, our work, our hobbies, our stage of life, and our relationships are just a few of the ways we identify ourselves.

In this study, we will spend time answering this question through a biblical lens as we discover who we are in Jesus. Who does He say we are? What titles and roles does He assign us? How does our relationship with Him impact our identity?

Today's reading comes from 2 Corinthians, a letter in the New Testament that was written by Paul to an early Christian church in a city called Corinth. In this section of his letter, Paul was encouraging the early church leaders to understand that they had not only been reconciled to God through the birth, death, and resurrection of Christ, but they were to see themselves—and other believers—as new creations.

It can be difficult to accept that someone we have known our whole lives has truly changed when we've only known them in one way. Paul was reminding the church, which includes us, not to focus on the outward identity of other believers but to focus on our new identity. In Jesus, we are a new creation. The old ways, thoughts, and motivations can be left in the past as we walk in freedom toward the next step in our journey in with Jesus.

PRAYER

Father God, thank You for sending Jesus to live and die and be raised again so I can become a new creation. I pray my words and actions would bring You glory so that I would be easily identified as Your child. Help me walk in freedom, leaving the old behind so I can fully embrace who You say I am. Amen.

READ

Ephesians 1:7–8

In him we have redemption through his blood, the forgiveness of our offenses, according to the riches of his grace 8 that he lavished on us in all wisdom and insight.

1 John 1:9

But if we confess our sins, he is faithful and righteous, forgiving us our sins and cleansing us from all unrighteousness.

SOAP

SOAP / *Ephesians 1:7*
SCRIPTURE / *Write out the SOAP verses*

_____

_____

_____

_____

_____

_____

_____

_____

_____

_____

_____

_____

_____

_____

_____

_____

_____

OBSERVATION / *Write 3 - 4 observations*

_____

_____

_____

_____

_____

_____

_____

_____

APPLICATION / *Write down 1 - 2 applications*

PRAYER / *Write out a prayer over what you learned*

SOAP

Ephesians 1:7

"In him we have redemption through his blood, the forgiveness of our offenses, according to the riches of his grace..."

INTO THE TEXT

Have you ever felt like your identity was wrapped and trapped in the mistakes of your past, instead of the hope of your future? Although most of us would never introduce ourselves to someone with a list of our failures and sins, we have probably found ourselves identifying others by what they've done and how they've hurt us, instead of who they really are.

When we take the time to explore what God's Word says about our identity, we discover He does not see us as the world sees us. He sees our hearts, and through the death of His Son on the cross, we can claim a new identity for ourselves when we accept Him as our Savior: forgiven.

We're not forgiven for only the small things, or forgiven only temporarily. When we ask God to forgive our sins, He forgives fully and completely. God will not bring up your past mistakes to use them against you or use them to define you. In Christ, we are forgiven.

Paul's letter to the Ephesians contains a beautiful portion of Scripture that scholars identify as a doxology. In Ephesians 1:3–14, Paul praised God while focusing our attention on the amazing things God has done for us. When we spend time remembering all God has done for us, the way He planned our redemption, all that was done to restore our relationship with Him, and the forgiveness we are offered through Jesus, our response should be gratitude and a willingness to offer that same love and forgiveness to others.

When we live as fully forgiven daughters of God, our hearts will overflow with gratitude for the gift God has given us, and we will be able to forgive ourselves and others.

PRAYER

God, thank You for the gift of forgiveness You offer through Jesus and the restoration it brings to my relationship with You. Help me to claim "forgiven" as part of my identity and to pass this gift along freely to others. Amen.

READ

Romans 5:1–2

Therefore, since we have been declared righteous by faith, we have peace with God through our LORD Jesus Christ, 2 through whom we have also obtained access into this grace in which we stand, and we rejoice in the hope of God's glory.

SOAP / *Romans 5:1–2*
SCRIPTURE / *Write out the SOAP verses*

_____

_____

_____

_____

_____

_____

_____

_____

_____

_____

_____

_____

_____

_____

_____

_____

_____

OBSERVATION / *Write 3 - 4 observations*

_____

_____

_____

_____

_____

_____

_____

_____

APPLICATION / *Write down 1 - 2 applications*

_____

_____

_____

_____

_____

_____

_____

_____

_____

_____

PRAYER / *Write out a prayer over what you learned*

_____

_____

_____

_____

_____

_____

_____

_____

_____

_____

_____

_____

_____

_____

_____

SOAP

Romans 5:1–2

"Therefore, since we have been declared righteous by faith, we have peace with God through our LORD Jesus Christ, through whom we have also obtained access into this grace in which we stand, and we rejoice in the hope of God's glory."

INTO THE TEXT

The dictionary defines "righteous" as being morally right or justified. We justify our actions by explaining our motives, or how it led to a positive outcome. We justify spending money or eating another slice of cake or going on vacation by trying to prove that we need or deserve it.

When we accept Jesus as our Savior, ask Him to forgive our sins, and commit our lives to Him, we are made righteous. Everything that separated us from God is covered by Jesus' sacrifice on the cross. We are not only made new, but we are made right before God.

In the earlier chapters of Paul's letter to the Romans, he explained our need for salvation and how we could receive salvation. In chapter 5, where our reading begins today, Paul explored the benefits we receive because of our salvation.

Peace. When we are made right with God through Jesus Christ, we experience the fruit of peace. Peace helps us live and act confidently because of what Jesus has done for us. This peace and confidence is not based on our circumstances or what we can achieve, but is real and lasting and only comes from Jesus.

Access. Layman's New Testament Bible Commentary notes the word used for "access" isn't simply an open door that we walk through, but "refers to ushering someone into the presence of royalty, or a ship sailing into the protection of a safe harbor." When we are made right before God, we are ushered into a place of protection, rest, and security.

PRAYER

Heavenly Father, thank You for loving me so much that You would create a way for me to be made right before You. You make me new, You forgive me, and You make a way so that I can come before You in peace and find rest. God, I praise You and love You. Amen.

READ

Psalm 107:1–3

Give thanks to the LORD, for he is good, and his loyal love endures. 2 Let those delivered by the LORD speak out, those whom he delivered from the power of the enemy, 3 and gathered from foreign lands, from east and west, from north and south.

Isaiah 43:1–3

Now, this is what the LORD says, the one who created you, O Jacob, and formed you, O Israel: "Don't be afraid, for I will protect you. I call you by name, you are mine. 2 When you pass through the waters, I am with you; when you pass through the streams, they will not overwhelm you. When you walk through the fire, you will not be burned; the flames will not harm you. 3 For I am the LORD your God, the Holy One of Israel, your deliverer. I have handed over Egypt as a ransom price, Ethiopia and Seba in place of you.

Romans 8:1–4

There is therefore now no condemnation for those who are in Christ Jesus. 2 For the law of the life–giving Spirit in Christ Jesus has set you free from the law of sin and death. 3 For God achieved what the law could not do because it was weakened through the flesh. By sending his own Son in the likeness of sinful flesh and concerning sin, he condemned sin in the flesh, 4 so that the righteous requirement of the law may be fulfilled in us, who do not walk according to the flesh but according to the Spirit.

SOAP / *Isaiah 43:1*
SCRIPTURE / *Write out the SOAP verses*

_____

_____

_____

_____

_____

_____

_____

_____

_____

_____

_____

_____

_____

_____

_____

OBSERVATION / *Write 3 - 4 observations*

_____

_____

_____

_____

_____

_____

_____

_____

APPLICATION / *Write down 1 - 2 applications*

PRAYER / *Write out a prayer over what you learned*

SOAP

Isaiah 43:1

"Now, this is what the LORD says, the one who created you, O Jacob, and formed you, O Israel: "Don't be afraid, for I will protect you. I call you by name, you are mine."

INTO THE TEXT

Knowing someone's name is significant. It means we have taken the time to get to know them, we've remembered them, and their name sets them apart from the other people we know. Using someone's name when we speak to them shows honor and respect. The nicknames we give our loved ones or close friends add a level of familiarity and care.

From the very beginning, you have been part of God's plan. He knows you, He cares for you, and He put into motion a series of events that would all lead up to His beautiful plan to redeem humanity. In our Scripture reading today we are reminded that God created us, formed us, protects us, knows our names, and calls us His.

Our identity as Christians is not based on what we have been able to accomplish, but on what has been freely done for us. In Jesus, we are redeemed through the great exchange of His life as payment for our sins.

We have been delivered (or redeemed), not by a distant God who puts all of humanity together, but a God who knows each of us by name. He knows you, He has a plan for you, He has given you gifts and skills and a specific place and time to use them for His kingdom. You are deeply loved by God – not as a number or a statistic or in general terms. He knows your name, and you are His.

PRAYER

God, it is overwhelming to think You know my name and care so personally about me. What an honor to be thought of and loved so much that You would call me Yours. It is through Your Son that I can claim my identity as a redeemed daughter of the King. Amen.

READ

2 Corinthians 1:21–22

But it is God who establishes us together with you in Christ and who anointed us, 22 who also sealed us and gave us the Spirit in our hearts as a down payment.

SOAP / *2 Corinthians 1:21–22*
SCRIPTURE / *Write out the SOAP verses*

_____
_____
_____
_____
_____
_____
_____
_____
_____
_____
_____
_____
_____
_____
_____
_____
_____
_____

OBSERVATION / *Write 3 - 4 observations*

_____
_____
_____
_____
_____
_____
_____
_____

APPLICATION / *Write down 1 - 2 applications*

PRAYER / *Write out a prayer over what you learned*

SOAP

2 Corinthians 1:21–22

"But it is God who establishes us together with you in Christ and who anointed us, who also sealed us and gave us the Spirit in our hearts as a down payment."

INTO THE TEXT

Have you ever picked up a package from the grocery store and noticed a warning that says, "Do not use if seal is broken"? Seals are placed on items to keep the contents on the inside away from anything harmful on the outside. Letters used to be sealed with wax for privacy, and important documents are sealed in envelopes today.

What does it mean that in Jesus we are sealed? In addition to seals providing security and protection, they were also used as a way to indicate ownership of an item. God is the one who establishes us with Christ, who anoints us, and who claims us as His. Our identity is secure in God, not because of the work we can do, but because the Holy Spirit is at work in us, sanctifying us, separating us from our past, and promising us a fully redeemed future.

Unlike seals on food or letters that can be tampered with, torn away, or melted, God's seal on us is secure. Our identity as a child of God is secure, with the Father, Son, and Holy Spirit all at work in us, through us, and for us, now and forever.

In 2 Corinthians 1:20, Paul wrote, "For every one of God's promises is 'yes' in him. Therefore, through him we also say 'amen' to the glory of God." Our identity is secure in God, and all of His promises are "yes"—they will happen, in His perfect timing and way—and "amen"—His promises are true, reliable, and will be established.

PRAYER

God, when the world tries to pick apart my identity and challenge who I think I am, remind me I am Yours. You have chosen me, established me, sealed me, and will keep Your promises to me. To You be all the glory and honor. Amen.

1. *How are you made a new creation in Christ? In what ways has Christ removed your old nature from your life and made you more like Him?*

....

....

....

2. *What does it mean that we are redeemed through the blood of Christ?*

....

....

....

3. *In what ways have you experienced Christ's forgiveness as you've confessed your sins to Him?*

....

....

....

4. *What does it mean to be righteous by faith? How does being righteous by faith give us peace?*

....

....

....

5. *What comfort do you find knowing that God knows you and calls you by name?*

....

....

....

JOURNAL
your thoughts

....
....
....
....
....
....
....
....
....
....
....
....
....
....
....
....
....
....
....
....
....
....
....
....
....

JOURNAL
your thoughts

....
....
....
....
....
....
....
....
....
....
....
....
....
....
....
....
....
....
....
....
....
....
....
....
....

But God, being
rich in mercy,
because of his
great love
with which he
loved us, even
though we were
dead in offenses,
made us alive
together with
Christ—by grace
you are saved!

Ephesians 2:4–5

*Write down your prayer requests
and praises for this week.*

....

....

....

....

....

....

....

....

....

....

....

....

WEEKLY CHALLENGE

*We are alive in Christ! In what ways has God made you alive? Reflect on the
ways God has restored your life spiritually, mentally, emotionally, physically, and
relationally.*

....

....

....

....

....

....

....

READ

John 3:16–17

16 For this is the way God loved the world: He gave his one and only Son, so that everyone who believes in him will not perish but have eternal life. 17 For God did not send his Son into the world to condemn the world, but that the world should be saved through him.

Colossians 1:11–14

being strengthened with all power according to his glorious might for the display of all patience and steadfastness, joyfully 12 giving thanks to the Father who has qualified you to share in the saints' inheritance in the light. 13 He delivered us from the power of darkness and transferred us to the kingdom of the Son he loves, 14 in whom we have redemption, the forgiveness of sins.

Hebrews 2:14–15

Therefore, since the children share in flesh and blood, he likewise shared in their humanity, so that through death he could destroy the one who holds the power of death (that is, the devil), 15 and set free those who were held in slavery all their lives by their fear of death.

SOAP / *Colossians 1:13*
SCRIPTURE / *Write out the SOAP verses*

_____

_____

_____

_____

_____

_____

_____

_____

_____

_____

_____

_____

_____

_____

_____

OBSERVATION / *Write 3 - 4 observations*

_____

_____

_____

_____

_____

_____

_____

_____

APPLICATION / *Write down 1 - 2 applications*

PRAYER / *Write out a prayer over what you learned*

SOAP

Colossians 1:13

"He delivered us from the power of darkness and transferred us to the kingdom of the Son he loves..."

INTO THE TEXT

Have you ever needed to be rescued? Maybe your car had a flat tire and you found yourself stranded on the side of the road, or you were temporarily stuck in an elevator when the power went out. It can be scary to feel stuck, unsure of when someone will arrive to offer assistance, how long you might have to wait, or how much it might cost.

In Jesus we are rescued. Not from flat tires or power outages, but from the enemy of our souls and an eternity in hell, separated from God because of our sin. Not only are we saved, we are fully rescued, moved from where we were to a new, safe, home in the kingdom of God, with no bill to pay back. We are fully rescued, paid in full.

Our identity in Christ is based on what God has done for us, not what we have done for ourselves or anyone else. The way we act, treat one another, the words we speak and the motivations in our hearts are a reflection of who we are in Christ. As the rescued, we now have eyes to see where help is needed so we can serve as the hands and feet of Jesus to those around us.

The more we learn about who God is, the better we understand who we are. And the more we understand and live out who we are as children of God, the more we will impact the lives of those around us in a way that draws others to the kingdom of God. The world's definition of identity puts the focus back on us, while understanding our identity in Christ gives us a vertical focus, back on God, and a horizontal focus to serve others.

No matter what you are facing today, no matter where you need God to step in and rescue you, He is faithful. He will deliver you.

PRAYER

Father God, my heart is overwhelmed at the fullness of the rescue You offer me. Thank You for moving me out of darkness and into the glorious light of eternity with You. Help me to use what I'm learning about who I am in You to serve those around me.

READ

Romans 5:8–10

But God demonstrates his own love for us, in that while we were still sinners, Christ died for us. 9 Much more then, because we have now been declared righteous by his blood, we will be saved through him from God's wrath. 10 For if while we were enemies we were reconciled to God through the death of his Son, how much more, since we have been reconciled, will we be saved by his life?

Ephesians 2:1–5

And although you were dead in your offenses and sins, 2 in which you formerly lived according to this world's present path, according to the ruler of the domain of the air, the ruler of the spirit that is now energizing the sons of disobedience, 3 among whom all of us also formerly lived out our lives in the cravings of our flesh, indulging the desires of the flesh and the mind, and were by nature children of wrath even as the rest...4 But God, being rich in mercy, because of his great love with which he loved us, 5 even though we were dead in offenses, made us alive together with Christ—by grace you are saved!—

SOAP / *Ephesians 2:4–5*
SCRIPTURE / *Write out the SOAP verses*

_____

_____

_____

_____

_____

_____

_____

_____

_____

_____

_____

_____

_____

_____

_____

_____

_____

OBSERVATION / *Write 3 - 4 observations*

_____

_____

_____

_____

_____

_____

_____

_____

APPLICATION / *Write down 1 - 2 applications*

_____
_____
_____
_____
_____
_____
_____
_____
_____
_____
_____

PRAYER / *Write out a prayer over what you learned*

_____
_____
_____
_____
_____
_____
_____
_____
_____
_____
_____
_____
_____
_____

SOAP

Ephesians 2:4–5

"But God, being rich in mercy, because of his great love with which he loved us, even though we were dead in offenses, made us alive together with Christ—by grace you are saved!"

INTO THE TEXT

There is something incredibly compelling about a "before and after" photo. Home renovations show us the potential we can find in our own rooms, while fitness transformations give us hope that our work will also pay off. It can be fun to look at photos that show others what we looked like in those awkward teenage years, or the difference between the start and end of a creative project.

In Paul's letter to the Ephesians, he spent time reminding them—and us—of the transformation that happens when we accept Jesus as our Savior. We are not only saved, but our identity shifts from "dead" to "alive." Paul wasn't speaking of a literal raising from the dead, but of the condition of our souls. Layman's New Testament Commentary describes it as "an existence devoid of the true purpose, character, and fulfillment of human life created in the image of God."

God loves us so much that He could not allow us to only have "death" as an option for our identity. When He planned our redemption through the sacrifice of His Son on the cross, we were given a new choice and a new identity: alive in Christ. When we understand who we were before Jesus came into our lives, we can appreciate even more the love, grace, and mercy God extends to each of us.

In Jesus we are saved, not only from the deserved punishment for our sins, but from our "before" identity to an "after" transformation that brings us to true, abundant life.

PRAYER

God, as I think about all the ways I don't deserve Your love, grace, and mercy, I am even more in awe of the gift of salvation You offer through Jesus. Thank You for giving me a new identity, an "after" that is full of life and hope and purpose. Amen.

READ

John 8:36

So if the son sets you free, you will be really free.

2 Corinthians 3:17

Now the LORD is the Spirit, and where the Spirit of the LORD is present, there is freedom.

SOAP / *John 8:36*
SCRIPTURE / *Write out the SOAP verses*

_____

_____

_____

_____

_____

_____

_____

_____

_____

_____

_____

_____

_____

_____

_____

OBSERVATION / *Write 3 - 4 observations*

_____

_____

_____

_____

_____

_____

_____

_____

APPLICATION / *Write down 1 - 2 applications*

_____

_____

_____

_____

_____

_____

_____

_____

_____

_____

_____

_____

PRAYER / *Write out a prayer over what you learned*

_____

_____

_____

_____

_____

_____

_____

_____

_____

_____

_____

_____

_____

_____

_____

SOAP

John 8:36

"So if the son sets you free, you will be really free."

INTO THE TEXT

Jesus was speaking to the Jews who had gathered in the temple in Jerusalem, a crowd who had mixed feelings about His identity as the Messiah. Those who did not believe pointed to the small town Jesus was from and His apparent lack of impressive family to discredit His claims (John 7:41–43). Little did they know, Jesus was about to fulfill every prophecy ever written about the coming Messiah!

In Jesus we are truly free. For a people who had experienced bondage and slavery as a nation, in a time when rulers and winners of battles enslaved their captives, they knew freedom as a fleeting opportunity. In John 8:35, Jesus reminded them that "the slave does not remain in the family forever, but the son remains forever." In Jesus, our identity is transformed from slave to son. We are offered full, complete, and permanent freedom—and a place in the family of God.

Although the world may attempt to limit our identity, influence, and impact because of our age, background, experience, or ability our identity is secure in Jesus. In Him, we are free. In Him, we have purpose. In Him, we become children of God and part of a family that will never leave us, doubt us, or run out of love for us. The chains of sin that have held us back are no longer effective against the power of Jesus Christ. We are free to be a light to those around us, a beacon of hope to our communities, and children of God who are secure in our identity no matter what comes our way.

PRAYER

Heavenly Father, thank You for inviting me to be part of Your family and setting me free from my sin. Help me live fully in freedom so others in my life might be drawn to You and Your beautiful gift of salvation. Amen.

READ

1 John 4:10–19

In this is love: not that we have loved God, but that he loved us and sent his Son to be the atoning sacrifice for our sins. 11 Dear friends, if God so loved us, then we also ought to love one another. 12 No one has seen God at any time. If we love one another, God resides in us, and his love is perfected in us. 13 By this we know that we reside in God and he in us: in that he has given us of his Spirit. 14 And we have seen and testify that the Father has sent the Son to be the Savior of the world. 15 If anyone confesses that Jesus is the Son of God, God resides in him and he in God. 16 And we have come to know and to believe the love that God has in us. God is love, and the one who resides in love resides in God, and God resides in him. 17 By this love is perfected with us, so that we may have confidence in the day of judgment, because just as Jesus is, so also are we in this world. 18 There is no fear in love, but perfect love drives out fear, because fear has to do with punishment. The one who fears punishment has not been perfected in love. 19 We love because he loved us first.

Romans 8:35–39

Who will separate us from the love of Christ? Will trouble, or distress, or persecution, or famine, or nakedness, or danger, or sword? 36 As it is written, "***For your sake we encounter death all day long; we were considered as sheep to be slaughtered.***" 37 No, in all these things we have complete victory through him who loved us! 38 For I am convinced that neither death, nor life, nor angels, nor heavenly rulers, nor things that are present, nor things to come, nor powers, 39 nor height, nor depth, nor anything else in creation will be able to separate us from the love of God in Christ Jesus our LORD.

SOAP / *1 John 4:10*
SCRIPTURE / *Write out the SOAP verses*

_____

_____

_____

_____

_____

_____

_____

_____

_____

_____

_____

_____

_____

_____

_____

_____

OBSERVATION / *Write 3 - 4 observations*

_____

_____

_____

_____

_____

_____

_____

_____

APPLICATION / *Write down 1 - 2 applications*

_____

_____

_____

_____

_____

_____

_____

_____

_____

_____

_____

PRAYER / *Write out a prayer over what you learned*

_____

_____

_____

_____

_____

_____

_____

_____

_____

_____

_____

_____

_____

_____

_____

SOAP

1 John 4:10

"In this is love: not that we have loved God, but that he loved us and sent his Son to be the atoning sacrifice for our sins."

INTO THE TEXT

In the English language, we only have one word for "love" and we use it dozens of ways. We say we love our new shoes, we love our spouse, we love the new book we borrowed from the library, and we love our favorite coffee. Love is often thought of as a feeling, an emotional response to something that brings us joy or delight. This also means love can be fleeting as our tastes change, our relationships shift, or things that used to bring us joy are replaced by something new.

God's definition of love is not based on what we feel, but what was revealed to us through Jesus' life and death. Love comes from God. Love came down to us from heaven in the physical presence of Jesus Christ, giving us a gift so unimaginable and undeserved that we could never do enough to earn it. It is simply and profoundly a gift from God.

First John 4:19 says, "we love because He first loved us." When our identity is firmly rooted in the knowledge that we are loved by the Creator of the universe, the love we show others comes from an overflow of what God has already done for us. This love will not change its mind and it is not dependent on what we can do to deserve it. God's love will not fail.

PRAYER

God, thank You for loving me and calling me Your beloved. As I claim "loved" as my identity in Jesus, help me share this love with others, especially those who feel hurt, alone, or abandoned. Yours is a perfect love, and I am so grateful for it. Amen.

READ

Romans 15:7–9

Receive one another, then, just as Christ also received you, to God's glory. 8 For I tell you that Christ has become a servant of the circumcised on behalf of God's truth to confirm the promises made to the fathers,9 and thus the Gentiles glorify God for his mercy. As it is written, "***Because of this I will confess you among the Gentiles, and I will sing praises to your name.***"

SOAP / *Romans 15:7*
SCRIPTURE / *Write out the SOAP verses*

OBSERVATION / *Write 3 - 4 observations*

APPLICATION / *Write down 1 - 2 applications*

_____

_____

_____

_____

_____

_____

_____

_____

_____

_____

PRAYER / *Write out a prayer over what you learned*

_____

_____

_____

_____

_____

_____

_____

_____

_____

_____

_____

_____

_____

_____

SOAP

Romans 15:7

*"Receive one another, then, just as Christ
also received you, to God's glory."*

INTO THE TEXT

As much as we all crave connection, a big part of our hearts also crave acceptance. An open door is nice, but a personal invitation and a seat saved for us at the table is better. When we feel accepted, we can come as we are, without the masks and without faking "fine."

In Paul's letter to the Romans, he encouraged the believers to receive—or accept—one another, the way they had been accepted by Jesus. Jesus receives us into His family already knowing the worst things we've ever done, said, or thought. He knows our past, present, and future, and He still makes a place for us with Him in eternity.

The early Roman Christians were struggling to accept other believers who did things a little differently, like the food they ate or the special days they observed. It was in these gray areas that some believers were starting to consider themselves better than others, judging their choices and practices. Paul was very clear in his letter that the only thing that would come out of this type of behavior was division.

In Jesus, we are received fully and completely into the family of God. Our differences make up a beautiful tapestry that brings life to the gospel. We are uniquely created in the image and likeness of God to use our gifts and talents to bring glory to God and grow His kingdom. If we are accepted with open arms by God, who are we to pass judgement on one another?

We need one another, and our witness to the gospel is hindered when we compete with and judge other believers. In Jesus we are not only received, but called to receive, accept, and support one another with open hearts.

PRAYER

Heavenly Father, even though I am a sinner who does not deserve Your love, You have chosen me and accepted me into Your family. Give me eyes to see those around me who do not know this acceptance so I can introduce them to You. Give me a heart to extend Your love without judgement. Amen.

1. How has Christ rescued your life from the power of darkness? How does it comfort you to know that He is always working for your deliverance, no matter the circumstance?

....

....

....

2. Because we are saved by grace, nothing we can do will change our status as a child of God. Do you believe this? Why or why not?

....

....

....

3. How has Christ given you freedom? What are you free from today that you were not free from before you were walking with Christ?

....

....

....

4. Did Christ love you before you loved Him? Why? What had you done to earn His love before you loved Him?

....

....

....

5. What does it mean to be received into the body of Christ? How can you receive and welcome others into the body of Christ?

....

....

....

JOURNAL
your thoughts

....
....
....
....
....
....
....
....
....
....
....
....
....
....
....
....
....
....
....
....
....
....
....
....
....

JOURNAL
your thoughts

....

....

....

....

....

....

....

....

....

....

....

....

....

....

....

....

....

....

....

....

....

....

....

....

....

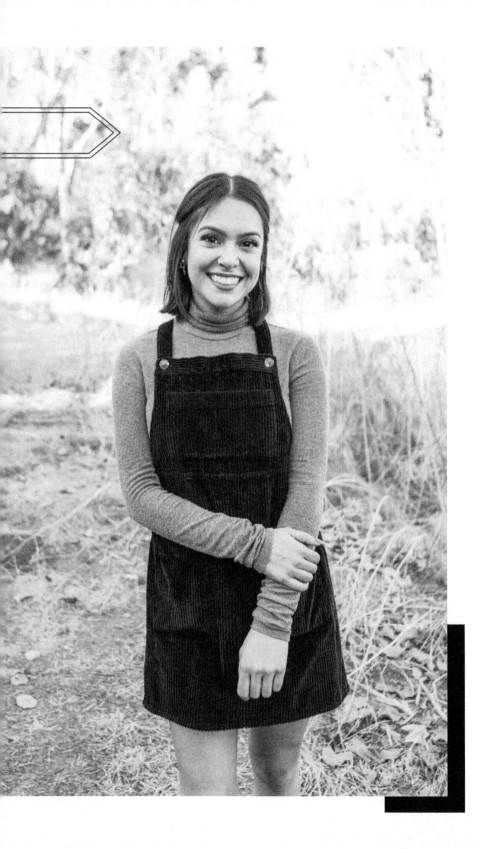

But our citizenship is in heaven, and we also eagerly await a savior from there, the Lord Jesus Christ.

Philippians 3:20

*Write down your prayer requests
and praises for this week.*

....

....

....

....

....

....

....

....

....

....

....

....

WEEKLY CHALLENGE

*This week, reflect on what it means to have citizenship in heaven. How does your
citizenship affect where you are able to live and work on earth? How does knowing
that, in Christ, you have eternal citizenship in heaven affect your life today?*

....

....

....

....

....

....

....

READ

Ephesians 1:5–6

He did this by predestining us to adoption as his legal heirs through Jesus Christ, according to the pleasure of his will— 6 to the praise of the glory of his grace that he has freely bestowed on us in his dearly loved Son.

Colossians 1:12–13

giving thanks to the Father who has qualified you to share in the saints' inheritance in the light. 13 He delivered us from the power of darkness and transferred us to the kingdom of the Son he loves,

SOAP

SOAP / *Ephesians 1:5*
SCRIPTURE / *Write out the SOAP verses*

OBSERVATION / *Write 3 - 4 observations*

APPLICATION / *Write down 1 - 2 applications*

_____

_____

_____

_____

_____

_____

_____

_____

_____

_____

_____

PRAYER / *Write out a prayer over what you learned*

_____

_____

_____

_____

_____

_____

_____

_____

_____

_____

_____

_____

_____

_____

_____

_____

SOAP

Ephesians 1:5

"He did this by predestining us to adoption as his legal heirs through Jesus Christ, according to the pleasure of his will—" Ephesians 1:5

INTO THE TEXT

Have you ever watched a video of a child learning they're going to be adopted, or witnessed the celebration of a family when a judge declares their adoption complete? It's one of the most beautiful, heartwarming moments. Despite the trauma and brokenness the child and their first family experienced, God provided a new way for family, for togetherness to exist. Suddenly a child's life is changed as they become a permanent, legal, complete member of a family. Adoption tells a child they are wanted, loved, and secure.

If you say your identity is "abandoned," "unwanted," "ignored," "overlooked," or "forgotten," there is good news—great news, in fact! When we accept Jesus as our Savior we get a new identity as adopted sons and daughters of God. You are chosen. You are wanted. You are known. You are loved. You are secure. No one has the power to undo what God has done. When we are adopted into the family of God we are His, forever.

The even better news is, God didn't wait for us to get our lives together or become perfect people before He decided to offer us the full rights, privileges, and responsibilities of believers. It was decided, in love and in accordance with God's will, that we would be adopted into His family through Jesus Christ.

When was the last time you embraced that identity? Have you come before God in amazement that He would choose you? Have you celebrated the amazing gift you've received through Jesus? God loves you so much, there isn't a "Welcome Home" sign big enough or confetti-filled enough to celebrate when you become part of His family. In Jesus, we are adopted!

PRAYER

God, it's overwhelming to know that You were thinking of me and planning a place for me in Your family before I ever knew Jesus. Thank You for the beautiful gift of adoption that You offer so freely. Help me live in a way that honors who You say I am. Amen.

READ

John 1:12

But to all who have received him—those who believe in his name—he has given the right to become God's children

1 John 3:1–2

See what sort of love the Father has given to us: that we should be called God's children—and indeed we are! For this reason the world does not know us: because it did not know him. 2 Dear friends, we are God's children now, and what we will be has not yet been revealed. We know that whenever it is revealed we will be like him, because we will see him just as he is.

SOAP / *John 1:12*
SCRIPTURE / *Write out the SOAP verses*

_____

_____

_____

_____

_____

_____

_____

_____

_____

_____

_____

_____

_____

_____

_____

_____

_____

OBSERVATION / *Write 3 - 4 observations*

_____

_____

_____

_____

_____

_____

_____

_____

APPLICATION / *Write down 1 - 2 applications*

PRAYER / *Write out a prayer over what you learned*

SOAP

John 1:12

"But to all who have received him—those who believe in his name—
he has given the right to become God's children." –John 1:12

INTO THE TEXT

When was the last time you played pretend or built a fort? Have you had a moment recently to let your imagination run wild, to laugh with your whole body, or make a mess in the name of creativity? Children see the world in an amazing way, as though everything in it is their playground. Items we see as trash become precious art supplies and silly games with no rules bring the loudest giggles.

Children live with open hearts and minds, ready to learn and willing to change. They rely on the adults in their lives to love them, keep them safe, and answer all the questions that come to mind when they should be getting ready for bed.

That's the relationship we're invited into when we become part of God's family. We are His children, and we receive not only the rights and privileges that come with our adoption, but a perfect Father who loves us, protects us, and listens to all of the questions that keep us awake at night. He is big enough to carry the weight of our worries so we can find freedom.

In Jesus, we are called children of God. If your experience with an earthly father makes it hard for you to lean into God the Father, bring all of that hurt and disappointment to Him. Spend time in God's Word and learn more about who He is and how much He loves you. Look for the small gifts He offers throughout your day and write down the little, ordinary ways He shows up in your life. Our God is unchanging and perfect. He made a place for you in His family—and that was not a mistake.

PRAYER

God, thank You for calling me Your child and for giving me a safe, perfect, loving place to come with all of my questions and worries. Help me find time to simply be child–like with You, laughing and creating and using my imagination freely and with joy. Amen.

READ

Ephesians 1:4

For he chose us in Christ before the foundation of the world that we should be holy and blameless before him in love.

1 Peter 2:9

But you are *a chosen race, a royal priesthood, a holy nation, a people of his own,* so that you may *proclaim the virtues* of the one who called you out of darkness into his marvelous light.

SOAP / *1 Peter 2:9*
SCRIPTURE / *Write out the SOAP verses*

_____

_____

_____

_____

_____

_____

_____

_____

_____

_____

_____

_____

_____

_____

OBSERVATION / *Write 3 - 4 observations*

_____

_____

_____

_____

_____

_____

_____

_____

APPLICATION / *Write down 1 - 2 applications*

_____

_____

_____

_____

_____

_____

_____

_____

_____

_____

PRAYER / *Write out a prayer over what you learned*

_____

_____

_____

_____

_____

_____

_____

_____

_____

_____

_____

_____

_____

_____

_____

SOAP

1 Peter 2:9

"But you are a chosen race, a royal priesthood, a holy nation, a people of his own, so that you may proclaim the virtues of the one who called you out of darkness into his marvelous light." 1 Peter 2:9

INTO THE TEXT

Our reading today contains some italicized lines that are important to explore as we look at our identity in Jesus. The author of our text, Peter, made a very specific point to quote several passages of Scripture from the Old Testament: Exodus 19:5–6, Isaiah 43:20–21, and Malachi 3:17. In the verses in Exodus, God told His people they would be a "kingdom of priests and a holy nation." In Isaiah we read God calls us His "chosen people" whom He created for His glory. In Malachi the God-of-Heaven's-Armies says we belong to Him.

It may have been easily understood by the Jews in the early church that they were God's chosen people, but Peter's message was a reminder that all Christians, including Gentiles, were chosen by God. That was new information for the early Christians, but it was important for the unity and identity of the church to understand that, in Jesus, we are all chosen by the One who called us out of darkness and into His light.

The truth shared with the early believers applies to us as well. Although the world may try to tell us we are insignificant, ordinary, or unwanted, we can claim a new identity in Jesus: chosen, royal, purposed, and called. When we remember all God has done for us and who we are in Him, our next step is to proclaim it to the world. Don't keep the Good News of the gospel to yourself; it's meant to be shared! The gospel is for everyone, and in Jesus, all are invited to step away from the darkness of their sin and into the marvelous light of forgiveness and eternity in heaven.

PRAYER

Lord, when I think about all You have done for me and who You say I am, it's nearly impossible to keep to myself. Put specific people on my heart this week who need to hear the Good News of the gospel so they, too, can be called chosen, holy, and saved. Amen.

READ

Ephesians 2:19

So then you are no longer foreigners and noncitizens, but you are fellow citizens with the saints and members of God's household,

Philippians 3:20

But our citizenship is in heaven—and we also eagerly await a savior from there, the LORD Jesus Christ,

SOAP / *Philippians 3:20*
SCRIPTURE / *Write out the SOAP verses*

OBSERVATION / *Write 3 - 4 observations*

APPLICATION / *Write down 1 - 2 applications*

PRAYER / *Write out a prayer over what you learned*

SOAP

Philippians 3:20

"But our citizenship is in heaven—and we also eagerly await a savior from there, the LORD Jesus Christ," – Philippians 3:20

INTO THE TEXT

When it comes to our identity, who we are is so much more than our name. We often describe someone by including their age, hair color, the work they do, the language they speak, and the country they're from. These details help us form a picture in our minds so we can have a shared understanding of who we're talking about, or to help us more easily identify someone if we're meeting them for the first time.

Throughout this study we've been learning that the identity God gives us is very different from the way the world describes us—and that is good news! God tells us we are His children, chosen, beloved, and forgiven. And when we believe in Jesus as our Savior we are also given a new citizenship in heaven!

The world's way of defining who we are creates separation and division from one another. It causes us to compare, compete, and think of ourselves more highly than someone else. The identity God gives us is always an invitation to inclusion and unity. When we are part of God's family, we all get to call heaven our home. His love extends to all of His children, and we are identified not by our accomplishments or success stories, but by the way we love one another.

In Jesus, we are citizens of heaven. We can rely on the hope we have in Him, that He is our Savior and He will come again one day. Until that day comes, when we can be with God for eternity, Paul's letter to the Philippians encourages us to stand firm in our faith. Hold tightly to who God says you are, live a life that bears good fruit and brings glory to the kingdom of God, and love others well.

PRAYER

God, thank You for giving me a fresh start when You forgave my sins, and for giving me a new identity, a new home, and a new hope. I pray my life would be a reflection of the love You have shown me so others might one day be able to claim their forever home in heaven with You. Amen.

READ

Psalm 139:1–3

O LORD, you examine me and know me. 2 You know when I sit down and when I get up; even from far away you understand my motives. 3 You carefully observe me when I travel or when I lie down to rest; you are aware of everything I do.

1 Corinthians 8:3

But if someone loves God, he is known by God.

SOAP

SOAP / *Psalm 139:1*
SCRIPTURE / *Write out the SOAP verses*

_____

_____

_____

_____

_____

_____

_____

_____

_____

_____

_____

_____

_____

_____

_____

_____

_____

_____

_____

OBSERVATION / *Write 3 - 4 observations*

_____

_____

_____

_____

_____

_____

_____

_____

_____

APPLICATION / *Write down 1 - 2 applications*

PRAYER / *Write out a prayer over what you learned*

SOAP

Psalm 139:1

"O LORD, you examine me and know me."

INTO THE TEXT

Take a moment to think about someone you know really well. Maybe it's your spouse, a parent, a sibling, or a best friend. Think about all the details you know about them, what they like and dislike, what their dreams are, their hobbies, what makes them laugh, and when the last time was that they cried.

No matter how well we know someone, we can never fully know them, not the way God knows His children. In our reading today, David used specific words to describe God's omniscience: know, understand, observe, and aware. God knew us, He knows us, and He will know us. He is not limited by time, and He is not restricted to only knowing us on a surface level.

David wrote in this psalm that God knows the big things about us, but also the small details of our days, like when we sit, stand, travel, or rest. God knows our words and the motive behind them, and there is nowhere we can possibly go where God is not with us.

Maybe you've had a relationship with someone and discovered the more you knew about them, the less you wanted to be around them. Maybe you've felt like you need to hide parts of your personality or the things you like in order to be accepted. In Jesus, we are fully known by God. He has examined us and still offers His love and protection. God will not leave you or forsake you because there is nothing about your life He doesn't already know—and He still invites you to be part of His family.

PRAYER

Lord, You know my past, my present, and my future, and You still make a place for me in Your family. As You examine me and know me, reveal anything in my heart that is keeping me from fully embracing my identity as a child of God so I can continue to grow closer to You. Amen.

REFLECT

1. *Being an adopted child of God means He can never disown you, no matter what you have done or may do. Do you believe this is true? Why or why not?*

....
....
....

2. *What does it mean to be a child of God? Do you find comfort in this truth? Why or why not?*

....
....
....

3. *Why has God chosen us to be His people? What does He ask us to do now that we are chosen as His?*

....
....
....

4. *How does knowing your citizenship is in heaven give you peace in your life today?*

....
....
....

5. *Are you comforted or frustrated knowing that God knows every detail and movement of your life? Why is it good that God knows everything about you?*

....
....
....

JOURNAL

your thoughts

....
....
....
....
....
....
....
....
....
....
....
....
....
....
....
....
....
....
....
....
....
....
....

JOURNAL

your thoughts

You are from
God, little
children, and
have conquered
them, because
the one who
is in you is
greater than
the one who is
in the world.

1 John 4:4

*Write down your prayer requests
and praises for this week.*

....

....

....

....

....

....

....

....

....

....

....

WEEKLY CHALLENGE

*In Christ, we have power over the enemy, and power over sin. How can you combat
the lies and schemes of the enemy this week, knowing that, in Christ, you are greater
than any enemy?*

....

....

....

....

....

....

....

READ

Psalm 139:13–18

Certainly you made my mind and heart; you wove me together in my mother's womb. 14 I will give you thanks because your deeds are awesome and amazing. You knew me thoroughly; 15 my bones were not hidden from you, when I was made in secret and sewed together in the depths of the earth. 16 Your eyes saw me when I was inside the womb. All the days ordained for me were recorded in your scroll before one of them came into existence. 17 How difficult it is for me to fathom your thoughts about me, O God! How vast is their sum total. 18 If I tried to count them, they would outnumber the grains of sand. Even if I finished counting them, I would still have to contend with you.

SOAP / *Psalm 139:13–14*
SCRIPTURE / *Write out the SOAP verses*

_____

_____

_____

_____

_____

_____

_____

_____

_____

_____

_____

_____

_____

_____

_____

OBSERVATION / *Write 3 - 4 observations*

_____

_____

_____

_____

_____

_____

_____

_____

_____

APPLICATION / *Write down 1 - 2 applications*

PRAYER / *Write out a prayer over what you learned*

SOAP

Psalm 139:13–14

"Certainly you made my mind and heart; you wove me together in my mother's womb. I will give you thanks because your deeds are awesome and amazing. You knew me thoroughly;"

INTO THE TEXT

Today's reading is a continuation of David's psalm that we read last week when we learned we are known by God. When we are known by Him, we can be certain our lives are not mere coincidence or fate–driven, but that we were created on purpose and for a purpose.

Certainly. It's a word that means without doubt, surely, and carries a feeling of agreement. We can confidently claim that in Jesus we are intentionally made because the Creator of the universe has formed us, knows us, and invites us into a relationship with Him. God made every part of you, not just the visible parts of your body but your feelings, personality, and talents. He carefully and purposefully fit it all together before you were even born, knowing exactly what kind of person you would become.

You are thoroughly and completely known by God. Your identity is secure in Him and your purpose is found in Him. David's psalm encourages us to respond to this knowledge of our identity with thanksgiving, not because of what we can do but because of what God has done. Who you are, where you are, and what you can do for God's kingdom is not random or a mistake. You were created with love and intention.

How can your life be a grateful reflection of this truth as you interact with others this week?

PRAYER

Heavenly Father, it is amazing to me that You carefully and intentionally formed every part of who I am, carefully weaving it all together before I was born. May my life reflect the gratitude I have for all You have done as I work, live, and love with purpose. Amen.

READ

Numbers 6:24–26

"The LORD bless you and protect you; 25 The LORD make his face to shine upon you, and be gracious to you; 26 The LORD lift up his countenance upon you and give you peace."'

2 Corinthians 9:8–10

And God is able to make all grace overflow to you so that because you have enough of everything in every way at all times, you will overflow in every good work. 9 Just as it is written, "*He has scattered widely, he has given to the poor; his righteousness remains forever.*" 10 Now God who provides seed for the sower and bread for food will provide and multiply your supply of seed and will cause the harvest of your righteousness to grow.

Ephesians 1:3

Blessed is the God and Father of our LORD Jesus Christ, who has blessed us with every spiritual blessing in the heavenly realms in Christ.

SOAP / *Ephesians 1:3*
SCRIPTURE / *Write out the SOAP verses*

OBSERVATION / *Write 3 - 4 observations*

APPLICATION / *Write down 1 - 2 applications*

_____
_____
_____
_____
_____
_____
_____
_____
_____
_____
_____

PRAYER / *Write out a prayer over what you learned*

_____
_____
_____
_____
_____
_____
_____
_____
_____
_____
_____
_____
_____
_____
_____

SOAP

Ephesians 1:3

"Blessed is the God and Father of our LORD Jesus Christ, who has blessed us with every spiritual blessing in the heavenly realms in Christ."

INTO THE TEXT

For many of us, to say we are "blessed" is often used to describe feeling lucky or to be glad we have obtained something we've been working toward. We'll say we're blessed to be given an opportunity, or we feel blessed a certain situation worked out in our favor. But in Paul's letter to the early church in Ephesus, the blessing he wrote about had nothing to do with luck and everything to do with the gifts we receive as believers.

God is blessed because He is holy, and it is only through the Father, Son, and Holy Spirit that we are able to be sealed, adopted, redeemed, and chosen. Those are the spiritual blessings we receive. We are also blessed with spiritual gifts and abilities to serve God's kingdom that flow out of the blessing we receive when we accept Christ as our Savior.

As citizens of heaven, created intentionally and fully known by God, our identity is rooted in Whose we are, not who we are. The gifts we receive from God are not by luck or fate or accident, but beautifully and purposefully planned out for our good and His glory. This opening portion of Paul's letter is considered a doxology, as Paul begins his message by first praising God for what He has done in a format that conveys worship and honor.

In Jesus we are blessed, not because of who we are or what we have done, but because our holy, amazing, wonderful God has chosen to bless us with gifts beyond anything we could ever ask or imagine.

PRAYER

God, You lavish gifts on Your children that are beyond anything I could ever imagine. May the words I speak, the thoughts I have, and the ways I use my gifts, all bring honor and glory to You as I remember and tell about the amazing things You have done. Amen.

READ

Ephesians 2:10

For we are his creative work, having been created in Christ Jesus for good works that God prepared beforehand so we can do them.

2 Timothy 3:16–17

Every scripture is inspired by God and useful for teaching, for reproof, for correction, and for training in righteousness, 17 that the person dedicated to God may be capable and equipped for every good work.

SOAP / *Ephesians 2:10*
SCRIPTURE / *Write out the SOAP verses*

_____

_____

_____

_____

_____

_____

_____

_____

_____

_____

_____

_____

_____

_____

_____

_____

_____

_____

OBSERVATION / *Write 3 - 4 observations*

_____

_____

_____

_____

_____

_____

_____

_____

APPLICATION / *Write down 1 - 2 applications*

PRAYER / *Write out a prayer over what you learned*

SOAP

Ephesians 2:10

"For we are his creative work, having been created in Christ Jesus for good works that God prepared beforehand so we can do them."

INTO THE TEXT

Children are wonderfully creative. They can see a pile of cardboard tubes and create telescopes, or turn a stack of blankets into a fort. Paint is meant to be messy, and coloring is best when it goes outside the lines. They look at clouds and see animal shapes and can create entire worlds and endless stories while playing with building blocks. Beauty isn't found in perfection, but in the experience.

As adults, it can be difficult to embrace our creativity. Our past experiences, doubts, and failures keep us from creating something simply for the sake of creating. If we are not able to do it perfectly, we wonder if we should even bother to do it at all. Beauty is found in the celebration and acceptance of what we produce, not in our enjoyment of the experience.

In Jesus we are equipped to do good works that God has prepared for us. We have been creatively designed to fulfill the plans and purpose He created specifically for us. What God created is beautiful. We can bring God glory and honor when we embrace who He made us to be and the work He designed for us to do.

God will equip us for the work, not because He knows we can do it perfectly, but because we are His creation, masterfully, intentionally, and creatively designed.

PRAYER

God, thank You for not only creating me, but giving me a purpose and equipping me to do the work You have designed for my life. You are endlessly creative, and I pray this week that I would find a way to create something beautiful, just for You, to honor who You say I am. Amen.

READ

1 Corinthians 12:4–11

Now there are different gifts, but the same Spirit. 5 And there are different ministries, but the same LORD. 6 And there are different results, but the same God who produces all of them in everyone. 7 To each person the manifestation of the Spirit is given for the benefit of all. 8 For one person is given through the Spirit the message of wisdom, and another the message of knowledge according to the same Spirit, 9 to another faith by the same Spirit, and to another gifts of healing by the one Spirit, 10 to another performance of miracles, to another prophecy, and to another discernment of spirits, to another different kinds of tongues, and to another the interpretation of tongues. 11 It is one and the same Spirit, distributing as he decides to each person, who produces all these things.

2 Corinthians 12:9

But he said to me, "My grace is enough for you, for my power is made perfect in weakness." So then, I will boast most gladly about my weaknesses, so that the power of Christ may reside in me.

Philippians 4:13

I am able to do all things through the one who strengthens me.

SOAP / *Philippians 4:13*
SCRIPTURE / *Write out the SOAP verses*

_____

_____

_____

_____

_____

_____

_____

_____

_____

_____

_____

_____

_____

_____

_____

_____

_____

OBSERVATION / *Write 3 - 4 observations*

_____

_____

_____

_____

_____

_____

_____

_____

APPLICATION / *Write down 1 - 2 applications*

PRAYER / *Write out a prayer over what you learned*

SOAP

Philippians 4:13

"I am able to do all things through the one who strengthens me."

INTO THE TEXT

We are constantly surrounded by the shouts of the world tell us that we can do anything and be anything that we want, as long as we work hard enough, try often enough, or buy enough stuff. We can earn that promotion at work on our own if we're simply better than everyone else. We can build a fabulous life for ourselves as long as we have enough, make enough, and surround ourselves with the right people.

In God's kingdom, we are at our strongest when we are weak, and we are our most independent when we are dependent on God. Our verse today does not mean that we should do all things, but that we can find joy as we rely on God to empower and equip us to do the work He calls us to do.

Paul took the time at the end of his letter to the church in Philippi to show his appreciation for their support of his ministry. He noted his joy came from the Lord, not from his circumstances. Although he had experienced times of need and times of abundance (Philippians 4:12), Paul shared that true contentment came from understanding his strength came from Jesus.

In Jesus, we are empowered to navigate all that life has for us through the strength we have in Him. When our joy and our identity are rooted in Christ, our circumstances will not shake us. Our consistent, joy–filled, lives will be a witness to the grace and love of Jesus who sustains us in all things and through all things.

PRAYER

Heavenly Father, the world tries to tell me I can do it all on my own, that in my own power I can do all things and be all things for all people. Help me quiet those shouts so I can fully depend on You to be my strength and my joy as You empower me to navigate all situations and circumstances in ways that bring You glory and honor. Amen.

READ

1 John 4:4

You are from God, little children, and
have conquered them, because the one
who is in you is greater than the one
who is in the world.

SOAP / *1 John 4:4*
SCRIPTURE / *Write out the SOAP verses*

_____

_____

_____

_____

_____

_____

_____

_____

_____

_____

_____

_____

_____

_____

_____

_____

_____

OBSERVATION / *Write 3 - 4 observations*

_____

_____

_____

_____

_____

_____

_____

_____

PRAYER / *Write out a prayer over what you learned*

SOAP

1 John 4:4

"You are from God, little children, and have conquered them, because the one who is in you is greater than the one who is in the world."

INTO THE TEXT

Through our time together in this study on identity, we have learned that who we are is not about anything we have done, but who God is and what He has done for us. When our identity is wrapped up in our location, vocation, or circumstances, we will be disappointed and discouraged when those things change. When we lean into an identity that is rooted firmly in who God says we are and what Jesus has done for us, what happens around us will not change or challenge our joy and peace.

The apostle John's letter to the early church was intended to remind believers of Jesus' true nature: fully God and fully human. False teachers had started to pop up, denying Jesus was the Messiah. First John encouraged us that we have already overcome these false teachers because the Holy Spirit is within us, helping us discern and conquer false teaching.

First John 4:4 reminds us of our identity as children of God. As God's children, we have been equipped with the Holy Spirit and unified with Christ. In Jesus we are: a new creation, forgiven, righteous, delivered, sealed, redeemed, saved, free, loved, received, adopted, chosen, known, intentionally made, blessed, equipped, and empowered. Our citizenship is in heaven with all of God's children and our identity offers unity with a community of believers—a gift far greater than the individualism and competition of the world.

You are who God says you are. You are His.

PRAYER

God, there are so many loud voices that try to pull me away from the truth of Your Word and who You say I am. Thank You for the gift of the Holy Spirit who helps me identify and conquer the lies so I can lean fully into my identity as a child of God. Amen.

1. *Are there aspects of your personality you are disappointed with or try to hide? How can you see yourself as intentionally created by God?*

....

....

....

2. *In what ways do you see God's blessing on your life? How has He given you every spiritual blessing in Christ?*

....

....

....

3. *What specific good works have you seen God equip and prepare you for? How have you seen Him work through your strengths and gifts to advance His kingdom or encourage others?*

....

....

....

4. *What does it mean that we are able to do all things through Christ? How can you find peace in your weakness or in difficult circumstances knowing He is always working, even in your weakness?*

....

....

....

5. *How are you empowered to fight against the enemy's schemes every day? How can you overcome the enemy through the power of Christ?*

....

....

....

JOURNAL
your thoughts

....

....

....

....

....

....

....

....

....

....

....

....

....

....

....

....

....

....

....

....

....

....

JOURNAL

your thoughts

....
....
....
....
....
....
....
....
....
....
....
....
....
....
....
....
....
....
....
....
....
....
....
....
....

SOAP it up between studies
2 week reading plan

Have you developed a consistent, daily Bible study habit
and don't want to break it before our next study begins?
In the following pages, you can continue your quiet
time with our suggested reading and SOAP passages.

WEEK 1

○ *Monday*
Reading: Psalm 101–102
SOAP: Psalm 102:1–2

○ *Tuesday*
Reading: Psalm 103–104
SOAP: Psalm 103:17–19

○ *Wednesday*
Reading: Psalm 105–106
SOAP: Psalm 106:44–45

○ *Thursday*
Reading: Psalm 107–108
SOAP: Psalm 107:1–3

○ *Friday*
Reading: Psalm 109–110
SOAP: Psalm 110:5–7

WEEK 2

○ *Monday*
Reading: Psalm 111–112
SOAP: Psalm 111:9

○ *Tuesday*
Reading: Psalm 113–114
SOAP: Psalm 113:4–6

○ *Wednesday*
Reading: Psalm 115–116
SOAP: Psalm 116:12

○ *Thursday*
Reading: Psalm 117–118
SOAP: Psalm 118:13–14

○ *Friday*
Reading: Psalm 119:1–40
SOAP: Psalm 119:15–16

O Lord, hear my prayer. Pay attention to my cry for help. Do not ignore me in my time of trouble. Listen to me. When I call out to you, quickly answer me.

Psalm 102:1-2

PRAY

*Write down your prayer requests
and praises for this week.*

....

....

....

....

....

....

....

....

....

....

....

....

....

....

....

....

....

....

....

....

....

....

....

....

READ

Psalm 101

A psalm of David.

1 I will sing about loyalty and justice.
To you, O Lord, I will sing praises.
2 I will walk in the way of integrity.
When will you come to me?
I will conduct my business with integrity
in the midst of my palace.
3 I will not even consider doing what is dishonest.
I hate doing evil;
I will have no part of it.
4 I will have nothing to do with a perverse person;
I will not permit evil.
5 I will destroy anyone who slanders
his neighbor in secret.
I will not tolerate anyone who has a haughty
demeanor and an arrogant attitude.
6 I will favor the honest people of the land,
and allow them to live with me.
Those who walk in the way of integrity will attend me.
7 Deceitful people will not live in my palace.
Liars will not be welcome in my presence.
8 Each morning I will destroy all the
wicked people in the land,
and remove all evildoers from the city of the Lord.
The prayer of an oppressed man, as he grows faint
and pours out his lament before the Lord.

Psalm 102

1 O Lord, hear my prayer.
Pay attention to my cry for help.
2 Do not ignore me in my time of trouble.
Listen to me.
When I call out to you, quickly answer me.
3 For my days go up in smoke,
and my bones are charred as in a fireplace.
4 My heart is parched and withered like grass,
for I am unable to eat food.
5 Because of the anxiety that makes me groan,
my bones protrude from my skin.
6 I am like an owl in the wilderness;
I am like a screech owl among the ruins.
7 I stay awake;
I am like a solitary bird on a roof.
8 All day long my enemies taunt me;
those who mock me use my name in their curses.
9 For I eat ashes as if they were bread,
and mix my drink with my tears,
10 because of your anger and raging fury.
Indeed, you pick me up and throw me away.
11 My days are coming to an end,
and I am withered like grass.
12 But you, O Lord, rule forever,
and your reputation endures.
13 You will rise up and have compassion on Zion.
For it is time to have mercy on her,
for the appointed time has come.
14 Indeed, your servants take delight in her stones,
and feel compassion for the dust of her ruins.
15 The nations will respect the
reputation of the Lord,

Psalm 102 (continued)

and all the kings of the earth will respect his splendor,
16 when the Lord rebuilds Zion,
and reveals his splendor,
17 when he responds to the prayer of the destitute,
and does not reject their request.
18 The account of his intervention will
be recorded for future generations;
people yet to be born will praise the Lord.
19 For he will look down from his sanctuary above;
from heaven the Lord will look toward earth,
20 in order to hear the painful cries of the prisoners,
and to set free those condemned to die,
21 so they may proclaim the name of the Lord in Zion,
and praise him in Jerusalem,
22 when the nations gather together,
and the kingdoms pay tribute to the Lord.
23 He has taken away my strength in the middle of life;
he has cut short my days.
24 I say, "O my God, please do not take
me away in the middle of my life.
You endure through all generations.
25 In earlier times you established the earth;
the skies are your handiwork.
26 They will perish,
but you will endure.
They will wear out like a garment;
like clothes you will remove them
and they will disappear.
27 But you remain;
your years do not come to an end.
28 The children of your servants will settle down here,
and their descendants will live securely in your presence."

SOAP / *Psalm 102:1–2*
SCRIPTURE / *Write out the SOAP verses*

_____

_____

_____

_____

_____

_____

_____

_____

_____

_____

_____

_____

_____

_____

_____

_____

_____

OBSERVATION / *Write 3 - 4 observations*

_____

_____

_____

_____

_____

_____

_____

_____

_____

APPLICATION / *Write down 1 - 2 applications*

_____
_____
_____
_____
_____
_____
_____
_____
_____
_____
_____

PRAYER / *Write out a prayer over what you learned*

_____
_____
_____
_____
_____
_____
_____
_____
_____
_____
_____
_____
_____
_____
_____
_____

THANKFUL

WEEK 1 • MONDAY

*Write three things you are thankful for
today and why each one brings you joy.*

ONE

....
....
....
....
....
....
....

TWO

....
....
....
....
....
....
....

THREE

....
....
....
....
....
....
....

READ

Psalm 103

By David.

1 Praise the Lord, O my soul.
With all that is within me, praise his holy name.
2 Praise the Lord, O my soul.
Do not forget all his kind deeds.
3 He is the one who forgives all your sins,
who heals all your diseases,
4 who delivers your life from the Pit,
who crowns you with his loyal love and compassion,
5 who satisfies your life with good things,
so your youth is renewed like an eagle's.
6 The Lord does what is fair,
and executes justice for all the oppressed.
7 The Lord revealed his faithful acts to Moses,
his deeds to the Israelites.
8 The Lord is compassionate and merciful;
he is patient and demonstrates great loyal love.
9 He does not always accuse,
and does not stay angry.
10 He does not deal with us as our sins deserve;
he does not repay us as our misdeeds deserve.
11 For as the skies are high above the earth,
so his loyal love towers over his faithful followers.
12 As far as the eastern horizon is from the west,
so he removes the guilt of our rebellious actions from us.
13 As a father has compassion on his children,
so the Lord has compassion on his faithful followers.
14 For he knows what we are made of;
he realizes we are made of clay.
15 A person's life is like grass.
Like a flower in the field it flourishes,
16 but when the hot wind blows, it disappears,
and one can no longer even spot the
place where it once grew.

Psalm 103 (continued)

17 But the LORD continually shows loyal
love to his faithful followers,
and is faithful to their descendants,
18 to those who keep his covenant,
who are careful to obey his commands.
19 The LORD has established his throne in heaven;
his kingdom extends over everything.
20 Praise the LORD, you angels of his,
you powerful warriors who carry out his decrees
and obey his orders.
21 Praise the LORD, all you warriors of his,
you servants of his who carry out his desires.
22 Praise the LORD, all that he has made,
in all the regions of his kingdom.
Praise the LORD, O my soul.

Psalm 104

1 Praise the LORD, O my soul!
O LORD my God, you are magnificent.
You are robed in splendor and majesty.
2 He covers himself with light as if it were a garment.
He stretches out the skies like a tent curtain,
3 and lays the beams of the upper rooms
of his palace on the rain clouds.
He makes the clouds his chariot,
and travels on the wings of the wind.
4 He makes the winds his messengers,
and the flaming fire his attendant.
5 He established the earth on its foundations;
it will never be moved.
6 The watery deep covered it like a garment;
the waters reached above the mountains.
7 Your shout made the waters retreat;
at the sound of your thunderous voice they hurried off—
8 as the mountains rose up,
and the valleys went down—

Psalm 104 (continued)

to the place you appointed for them.
9 You set up a boundary for them
that they could not cross,
so that they would not cover the earth again.
10 He turns springs into streams;
they flow between the mountains.
11 They provide water for all the animals in the field;
the wild donkeys quench their thirst.
12 The birds of the sky live beside them;
they chirp among the bushes.
13 He waters the mountains from the
upper rooms of his palace;
the earth is full of the fruit you cause to grow.
14 He provides grass for the cattle,
and crops for people to cultivate,
so they can produce food from the ground,
15 as well as wine that makes people glad,
and olive oil to make their faces shine,
as well as bread that sustains them.
16 The trees of the LORD receive all the rain they need,
the cedars of Lebanon that he planted,
17 where the birds make nests,
near the evergreens in which the herons live.
18 The wild goats live in the high mountains;
the rock badgers find safety in the cliffs.
19 He made the moon to mark the months,
and the sun sets according to a regular schedule.
20 You make it dark and night comes,
during which all the beasts of the forest prowl around.
21 The lions roar for prey,
seeking their food from God.
22 When the sun rises, they withdraw
and sleep in their dens.
23 People then go out to do their work,
and they labor until evening.
24 How many living things you have made, O LORD!
You have exhibited great skill in making all of them;

Psalm 104 (continued)

the earth is full of the living things you have made.
25 Over here is the deep, wide sea,
which teems with innumerable swimming creatures,
living things both small and large.
26 The ships travel there,
and over here swims the whale you made to play in it.
27 All your creatures wait for you
to provide them with food on a regular basis.
28 You give food to them and they receive it;
you open your hand and they are filled with food.
29 When you ignore them, they panic.
When you take away their life's breath,
they die and return to dust.
30 When you send your life–giving
breath, they are created,
and you replenish the surface of the ground.
31 May the splendor of the LORD endure.
May the LORD find pleasure in the
living things he has made.
32 He looks down on the earth and it shakes;
he touches the mountains and they start to smolder.
33 I will sing to the LORD as long as I live;
I will sing praise to my God as long as I exist.
34 May my thoughts be pleasing to him.
I will rejoice in the LORD.
35 May sinners disappear from the earth,
and the wicked vanish.
Praise the LORD, O my soul.
Praise the LORD.

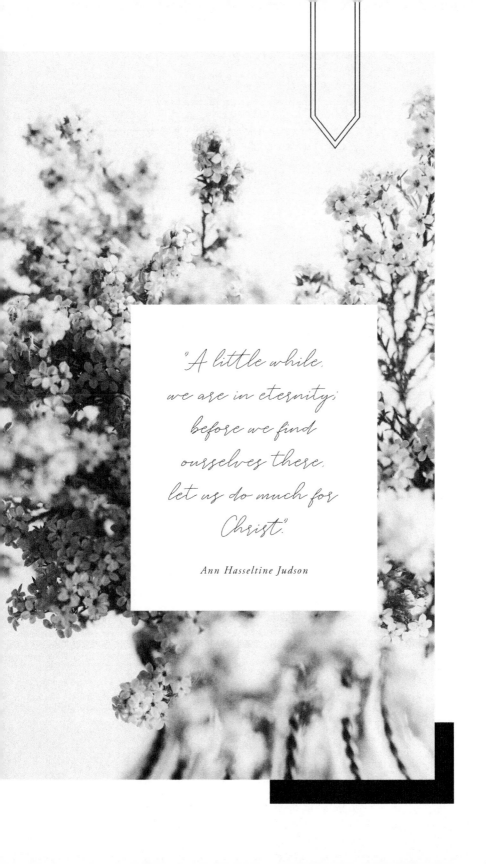

"A little while,
we are in eternity;
before we find
ourselves there,
let us do much for
Christ."

Ann Hasseltine Judson

SOAP / *Psalm 103:17–19*
SCRIPTURE / *Write out the SOAP verses*

OBSERVATION / *Write 3 - 4 observations*

APPLICATION / *Write down 1 - 2 applications*

PRAYER / *Write out a prayer over what you learned*

THANKFUL
WEEK 1 · TUESDAY

Write three things you are thankful for
today and why each one brings you joy.

ONE

....
....
....
....
....
....
....

TWO

....
....
....
....
....
....
....

THREE

....
....
....
....
....
....
....

READ

Psalm 105

1 Give thanks to the LORD.
Call on his name.
Make known his accomplishments among the nations.
2 Sing to him.
Make music to him.
Tell about all his miraculous deeds.
3 Boast about his holy name.
Let the hearts of those who seek the LORD rejoice.
4 Seek the LORD and the strength he gives.
Seek his presence continually.
5 Recall the miraculous deeds he performed,
his mighty acts and the judgments he decreed,
6 O children of Abraham, God's servant,
you descendants of Jacob, God's chosen ones.
7 He is the LORD our God;
he carries out judgment throughout the earth.
8 He always remembers his covenantal decree,
the promise he made to a thousand generations—
9 the promise he made to Abraham,
the promise he made by oath to Isaac.
10 He gave it to Jacob as a decree,
to Israel as a lasting promise,
11 saying, "To you I will give the land of Canaan
as the portion of your inheritance."
12 When they were few in number,
just a very few, and resident foreigners within it,
13 they wandered from nation to nation,
and from one kingdom to another.
14 He let no one oppress them;
he disciplined kings for their sake,
15 saying, "Don't touch my chosen ones.
Don't harm my prophets."
16 He called down a famine upon the earth;
he cut off all the food supply.
17 He sent a man ahead of them—
Joseph was sold as a servant.
18 The shackles hurt his feet;
his neck was placed in an iron collar,

Psalm 105 (continued)

19 until the time when his prediction came true.
The LORD's word proved him right.
20 The king authorized his release;
the ruler of nations set him free.
21 He put him in charge of his palace,
and made him manager of all his property,
22 giving him authority to imprison his officials
and to teach his advisers.
23 Israel moved to Egypt;
Jacob lived for a time in the land of Ham.
24 The LORD made his people very fruitful,
and made them more numerous than their enemies.
25 He caused the Egyptians to hate his people,
and to mistreat his servants.
26 He sent his servant Moses,
and Aaron, whom he had chosen.
27 They executed his miraculous signs among them,
and his amazing deeds in the land of Ham.
28 He made it dark;
Moses and Aaron did not disobey his orders.
29 He turned the Egyptians' water into blood,
and killed their fish.
30 Their land was overrun by frogs,
which even got into the rooms of their kings.
31 He ordered flies to come;
gnats invaded their whole territory.
32 He sent hail along with the rain;
there was lightning in their land.
33 He destroyed their vines and fig trees,
and broke the trees throughout their territory.
34 He ordered locusts to come,
innumerable grasshoppers.
35 They ate all the vegetation in their land,
and devoured the crops of their fields.
36 He struck down all the firstborn in their land,
the firstfruits of their reproductive power.
37 He brought his people out enriched with silver and gold;
none of his tribes stumbled.
38 Egypt was happy when they left,
for they were afraid of them.
39 He spread out a cloud for a cover,

Psalm 105 (continued)

and provided a fire to light up the night.
40 They asked for food, and he sent quail;
he satisfied them with food from the sky.
41 He opened up a rock and water flowed out;
a river ran through dry regions.
42 Yes, he remembered the sacred promise
he made to Abraham his servant.
43 When he led his people out, they rejoiced;
his chosen ones shouted with joy.
44 He handed the territory of nations over to them,
and they took possession of what other peoples had produced,
45 so that they might keep his commands
and obey his laws.
Praise the LORD.

Psalm 106

1 Praise the LORD.
Give thanks to the LORD, for he is good,
and his loyal love endures.
2 Who can adequately recount the LORD's mighty acts,
or relate all his praiseworthy deeds?
3 How blessed are those who promote justice,
and do what is right all the time.
4 Remember me, O LORD, when you show favor to your people.
Pay attention to me, when you deliver,
5 so I may see the prosperity of your chosen ones,
rejoice along with your nation,
and boast along with the people who belong to you.
6 We have sinned like our ancestors;
we have done wrong, we have done evil.
7 Our ancestors in Egypt failed to appreciate your miraculous deeds.
They failed to remember your many acts of loyal love,
and they rebelled at the sea, by the Red Sea.
8 Yet he delivered them for the sake of his reputation,
that he might reveal his power.
9 He shouted at the Red Sea and it dried up;
he led them through the deep water as if it were a desert.
10 He delivered them from the power of the one who hated them,
and rescued them from the power of the enemy.
11 The water covered their enemies;

Psalm 106 (continued)

not even one of them survived.
12 They believed his promises;
they sang praises to him.
13 They quickly forgot what he had done;
they did not wait for his instructions.
14 In the wilderness they had an insatiable craving for meat;
they challenged God in the wastelands.
15 He granted their request,
then struck them with a disease.
16 In the camp they resented Moses,
and Aaron, the LORD's holy priest.
17 The earth opened up and swallowed Dathan;
it engulfed the group led by Abiram.
18 Fire burned their group;
the flames scorched the wicked.
19 They made an image of a calf at Horeb,
and worshiped a metal idol.
20 They traded their majestic God
for the image of an ox that eats grass.
21 They rejected the God who delivered them,
the one who performed great deeds in Egypt,
22 amazing feats in the land of Ham,
mighty acts by the Red Sea.
23 He threatened to destroy them,
but Moses, his chosen one, interceded with him
and turned back his destructive anger.
24 They rejected the fruitful land;
they did not believe his promise.
25 They grumbled in their tents;
they did not obey the LORD.
26 So he made a solemn vow
that he would make them die in the wilderness,
27 make their descendants die among the nations,
and scatter them among foreign lands.
28 They worshiped Baal of Peor,
and ate sacrifices offered to the dead.
29 They made the LORD angry by their actions,
and a plague broke out among them.
30 Phinehas took a stand and intervened,
and the plague subsided.
31 This was credited to Phinehas as a righteous act

Psalm 106 (continued)

for all generations to come.
32 They made him angry by the waters of Meribah,
and Moses suffered because of them,
33 for they aroused his temper,
and he spoke rashly.
34 They did not destroy the nations,
as the Lord had commanded them to do.
35 They mixed in with the nations
and learned their ways.
36 They worshiped their idols,
which became a snare to them.
37 They sacrificed their sons and
daughters to demons.
38 They shed innocent blood—
the blood of their sons and daughters,
whom they sacrificed to the idols of Canaan.
The land was polluted by bloodshed.
39 They were defiled by their deeds,
and unfaithful in their actions.
40 So the Lord was angry with his people
and despised the people who belonged to him.
41 He handed them over to the nations,
and those who hated them ruled over them.
42 Their enemies oppressed them;
they were subject to their authority.
43 Many times he delivered them,
but they had a rebellious attitude,
and degraded themselves by their sin.
44 Yet he took notice of their distress,
when he heard their cry for help.
45 He remembered his covenant with them,
and relented because of his great loyal love.
46 He caused all their conquerors
to have pity on them.
47 Deliver us, O Lord, our God.
Gather us from among the nations.
Then we will give thanks to your holy name,
and boast about your praiseworthy deeds.
48 The Lord God of Israel deserves praise,
in the future and forevermore.
Let all the people say, "We agree! Praise the Lord!"

SOAP / *Psalm 106:44–45*
SCRIPTURE / *Write out the SOAP verses*

_____

_____

_____

_____

_____

_____

_____

_____

_____

_____

_____

_____

_____

_____

_____

OBSERVATION / *Write 3 - 4 observations*

_____

_____

_____

_____

_____

_____

_____

_____

APPLICATION / *Write down 1 - 2 applications*

PRAYER / *Write out a prayer over what you learned*

THANKFUL

*Write three things you are thankful for
today and why each one brings you joy.*

ONE

....
....
....
....
....
....
....

TWO

....
....
....
....
....
....
....

THREE

....
....
....
....
....
....
....

READ

Psalm 107

1 Give thanks to the LORD, for he is good,
and his loyal love endures.
2 Let those delivered by the LORD speak out,
those whom he delivered from the power of the enemy,
3 and gathered from foreign lands,
from east and west, from north and south.
4 They wandered through the wilderness, in a wasteland;
they found no road to a city in which to live.
5 They were hungry and thirsty;
they fainted from exhaustion.
6 They cried out to the LORD in their distress;
he delivered them from their troubles.
7 He led them on a level road,
that they might find a city in which to live.
8 Let them give thanks to the LORD for his loyal love,
and for the amazing things he has done for people.
9 For he has satisfied those who thirst,
and those who hunger he has filled with food.
10 They sat in utter darkness,
bound in painful iron chains,
11 because they had rebelled against God's commands,
and rejected the instructions of the Most High.
12 So he used suffering to humble them;
they stumbled and no one helped them up.
13 They cried out to the LORD in their distress;
he delivered them from their troubles.
14 He brought them out of the utter darkness,
and tore off their shackles.
15 Let them give thanks to the LORD for his loyal love,
and for the amazing things he has done for people.
16 For he shattered the bronze gates,
and hacked through the iron bars.
17 They acted like fools in their rebellious ways,
and suffered because of their sins.
18 They lost their appetite for all food,
and they drew near the gates of death.
19 They cried out to the LORD in their distress;
he delivered them from their troubles.
20 He sent them an assuring word and healed them;

Psalm 107 (continued)

he rescued them from the pits where they were trapped.
21 Let them give thanks to the LORD for his loyal love,
and for the amazing things he has done for people.
22 Let them present thank offerings,
and loudly proclaim what he has done.
23 Some traveled on the sea in ships,
and carried cargo over the vast waters.
24 They witnessed the acts of the LORD,
his amazing feats on the deep water.
25 He gave the order for a windstorm,
and it stirred up the waves of the sea.
26 They reached up to the sky,
then dropped into the depths.
The sailors' strength left them because the danger was so great.
27 They swayed and staggered like drunks,
and all their skill proved ineffective.
28 They cried out to the LORD in their distress;
he delivered them from their troubles.
29 He calmed the storm, and the waves grew silent.
30 The sailors rejoiced because the waves grew quiet,
and he led them to the harbor they desired.
31 Let them give thanks to the LORD for his loyal love,
and for the amazing things he has done for people.
32 Let them exalt him in the assembly of the people.
Let them praise him in the place where the leaders preside.
33 He turned streams into a desert,
springs of water into arid land,
34 and a fruitful land into a barren place,
because of the sin of its inhabitants.
35 As for his people, he turned a desert into a pool of water,
and a dry land into springs of water.
36 He allowed the hungry to settle there,
and they established a city in which to live.
37 They cultivated fields, and planted vineyards,
which yielded a harvest of fruit.
38 He blessed them so that they became very numerous.
He would not allow their cattle to decrease in number.
39 As for their enemies, they decreased in
number and were beaten down,
because of painful distress and suffering.
40 He would pour contempt upon princes,

Psalm 107 (continued)

and he made them wander in a wasteland with no road.
41 Yet he protected the needy from oppression,
and cared for his families like a flock of sheep.
42 When the godly see this, they rejoice,
and every sinner shuts his mouth.
43 Whoever is wise, let him take note of these things.
Let them consider the LORD's acts of loyal love.

Psalm 108

A song, a psalm of David.

1 I am determined, O God.
I will sing and praise you with my whole heart.
2 Awake, O stringed instrument and harp.
I will wake up at dawn.
3 I will give you thanks before the nations, O LORD.
I will sing praises to you before foreigners.
4 For your loyal love extends beyond the sky,
and your faithfulness reaches the clouds.
5 Rise up above the sky, O God.
May your splendor cover the whole earth.
6 Deliver by your power and answer me,
so that the ones you love may be safe.
7 God has spoken in his sanctuary:
"I will triumph! I will parcel out Shechem;
the Valley of Sukkoth I will measure off.
8 Gilead belongs to me, as does Manasseh.
Ephraim is my helmet, Judah my royal scepter.
9 Moab is my washbasin.
I will make Edom serve me.
I will shout in triumph over Philistia."
10 Who will lead me into the fortified city?
Who will bring me to Edom?
11 Have you not rejected us, O God?
O God, you do not go into battle with our armies.
12 Give us help against the enemy,
for any help men might offer is futile.
13 By God's power we will conquer;
he will trample down our enemies.

SOAP / *Psalm 107:1–3*
SCRIPTURE / *Write out the SOAP verses*

OBSERVATION / *Write 3 - 4 observations*

APPLICATION / *Write down 1 - 2 applications*

PRAYER / *Write out a prayer over what you learned*

THANKFUL

*Write three things you are thankful for
today and why each one brings you joy.*

ONE

....
....
....
....
....
....
....

TWO

....
....
....
....
....
....
....

THREE

....
....
....
....
....
....
....

READ

Psalm 109

For the music director, a psalm of David.

1 O God whom I praise, do not ignore me.
2 For they say cruel and deceptive things to me;
they lie to me.
3 They surround me and say hateful things;
they attack me for no reason.
4 They repay my love with accusations,
but I continue to pray.
5 They repay me evil for good,
and hate for love.
6 Appoint an evil man to testify against him.
May an accuser stand at his right side.
7 When he is judged, he will be found guilty.
Then his prayer will be regarded as sinful.
8 May his days be few.
May another take his job.
9 May his children be fatherless,
and his wife a widow.
10 May his children roam around begging,
asking for handouts as they leave their ruined home.
11 May the creditor seize all he owns.
May strangers loot his property.
12 May no one show him kindness.
May no one have compassion on his fatherless children.
13 May his descendants be cut off.
May the memory of them be wiped out by
the time the next generation arrives.
14 May his ancestors' sins be remembered by the Lord.
May his mother's sin not be forgotten.
15 May the Lord be constantly aware of them,
and cut off the memory of his children from the earth.
16 For he never bothered to show kindness;
he harassed the oppressed and needy,
and killed the disheartened.

Psalm 109 (continued)

17 He loved to curse others, so those
curses have come upon him.
He had no desire to bless anyone, so
he has experienced no blessings.
18 He made cursing a way of life,
so curses poured into his stomach like water
and seeped into his bones like oil.
19 May a curse attach itself to him,
like a garment one puts on,
or a belt one wears continually.
20 May the LORD repay my accusers in this way,
those who say evil things about me.
21 O Sovereign LORD,
intervene on my behalf for the sake of your reputation.
Because your loyal love is good, deliver me.
22 For I am oppressed and needy,
and my heart beats violently within me.
23 I am fading away like a shadow at the end of the day;
I am shaken off like a locust.
24 I am so starved my knees shake;
I have turned into skin and bones.
25 I am disdained by them.
When they see me, they shake their heads.
26 Help me, O LORD my God.
Because you are faithful to me, deliver me.
27 Then they will realize this is your work,
and that you, LORD, have accomplished it.
28 They curse, but you will bless.
When they attack, they will be humiliated,
but your servant will rejoice.
29 My accusers will be covered with shame,
and draped in humiliation as if it were a robe.
30 I will thank the LORD profusely.
In the middle of a crowd I will praise him,
31 because he stands at the right hand of the needy,
to deliver him from those who threaten his life.

Psalm 110

A psalm of David.

1 Here is the LORD's proclamation to my lord:
"Sit down at my right hand until I make
your enemies your footstool."
2 The LORD extends your dominion from Zion.
Rule in the midst of your enemies.
3 Your people willingly follow
you when you go into battle.
On the holy hills at sunrise the dew
of your youth belongs to you.
4 The LORD makes this promise on
oath and will not revoke it:
"You are an eternal priest after the
pattern of Melchizedek."
5 O LORD, at your right hand
he strikes down kings in the day he unleashes his anger.
6 He executes judgment against the nations.
He fills the valleys with corpses;
he shatters their heads over the vast battlefield.
7 From the stream along the road he drinks;
then he lifts up his head.

SOAP / *Psalm 110:5–7*
SCRIPTURE / *Write out the SOAP verses*

OBSERVATION / *Write 3 - 4 observations*

APPLICATION / *Write down 1 - 2 applications*

PRAYER / *Write out a prayer over what you learned*

THANKFUL

*Write three things you are thankful for
today and why each one brings you joy.*

ONE

....
....
....
....
....
....
....

TWO

....
....
....
....
....
....
....

THREE

....
....
....
....
....
....
....

REFLECT

Record an application you learned from your SOAP study this week and how you will practically implement it in your life.

....

....

....

....

....

....

....

....

....

....

....

....

....

....

....

....

....

....

....

....

....

....

....

....

JOURNAL

your thoughts

....
....
....
....
....
....
....
....
....
....
....
....
....
....
....
....
....
....
....
....
....
....
....
....
....

The Lord
gives me
strength
and protects
me; he has
become my
deliverer

Psalm 118:14

PRAY

*Write down your prayer requests
and praises for this week.*

....
....
....
....
....
....
....
....
....
....
....
....
....
....
....
....
....
....
....
....
....
....
....
....

READ

Psalm 111

1 Praise the LORD!
I will give thanks to the LORD with my whole heart,
in the assembly of the godly and the congregation.
2 The LORD's deeds are great,
eagerly awaited by all who desire them.
3 His work is majestic and glorious,
and his faithfulness endures forever.
4 He does amazing things that will be remembered;
the LORD is merciful and compassionate.
5 He gives food to his faithful followers;
he always remembers his covenant.
6 He announced that he would do
mighty deeds for his people,
giving them a land that belonged to other nations.
7 His acts are characterized by faithfulness and justice;
all his precepts are reliable.
8 They are forever firm,
and should be faithfully and properly carried out.
9 He delivered his people;
he ordained that his covenant be observed forever.
His name is holy and awesome.
10 To obey the LORD is the fundamental
principle for wise living;
all who carry out his precepts acquire good moral insight.
He will receive praise forever.

Psalm 112

1 Praise the LORD!
How blessed is the one who obeys the LORD,
who takes great delight in keeping his commands.
2 His descendants will be powerful on the earth;
the godly will be blessed.
3 His house contains wealth and riches;
his integrity endures.
4 In the darkness a light shines for the godly,
for each one who is merciful, compassionate, and just.
5 It goes well for the one who generously lends money,
and conducts his business honestly.
6 For he will never be shaken;
others will always remember one who is just.
7 He does not fear bad news.
He is confident; he trusts in the LORD.
8 His resolve is firm; he will not succumb to fear
before he looks in triumph on his enemies.
9 He generously gives to the needy;
his integrity endures.
He will be vindicated and honored.
10 When the wicked see this, they will worry;
they will grind their teeth in frustration and melt away.
The desire of the wicked will perish.

"It is our work to cast care, and it is God's work to take care."

Thomas Watson

SOAP / *Psalm 111:9*
SCRIPTURE / *Write out the SOAP verses*

_____

_____

_____

_____

_____

_____

_____

_____

_____

_____

_____

_____

_____

_____

_____

_____

_____

OBSERVATION / *Write 3 - 4 observations*

_____

_____

_____

_____

_____

_____

_____

_____

APPLICATION / *Write down 1 - 2 applications*

PRAYER / *Write out a prayer over what you learned*

THANKFUL

Write three things you are thankful for today and why each one brings you joy.

ONE

....
....
....
....
....
....
....

TWO

....
....
....
....
....
....
....

THREE

....
....
....
....
....
....
....

READ

Psalm 113

1 Praise the Lord.
Praise, you servants of the Lord,
praise the name of the Lord.
2 May the Lord's name be praised
now and forevermore.
3 From east to west
the Lord's name is deserving of praise.
4 The Lord is exalted over all the nations;
his splendor reaches beyond the sky.
5 Who can compare to the Lord our God,
who sits on a high throne?
6 He bends down to look
at the sky and the earth.
7 He raises the poor from the dirt,
and lifts up the needy from the garbage pile,
8 that he might seat him with princes,
with the princes of his people.
9 He makes the barren woman of the family
a happy mother of children.
Praise the Lord.

Psalm 114

1 When Israel left Egypt,
when the family of Jacob left a foreign nation behind,
2 Judah became his sanctuary,
Israel his kingdom.
3 The sea looked and fled;
the Jordan River turned back.
4 The mountains skipped like rams,
the hills like lambs.
5 Why do you flee, O sea?
Why do you turn back, O Jordan River?
6 Why do you skip like rams, O mountains,
like lambs, O hills?
7 Tremble, O earth, before the Lord—
before the God of Jacob,
8 who turned a rock into a pool of water,
a hard rock into springs of water.

SOAP / *Psalm 113:4–6*
SCRIPTURE / *Write out the SOAP verses*

_____

_____

_____

_____

_____

_____

_____

_____

_____

_____

_____

_____

_____

_____

_____

_____

OBSERVATION / *Write 3 - 4 observations*

_____

_____

_____

_____

_____

_____

_____

_____

APPLICATION / *Write down 1 - 2 applications*

PRAYER / *Write out a prayer over what you learned*

THANKFUL

*Write three things you are thankful for
today and why each one brings you joy.*

ONE

....

....

....

....

....

....

....

TWO

....

....

....

....

....

....

....

THREE

....

....

....

....

....

....

....

READ

Psalm 115

1 Not to us, O LORD, not to us,
but to your name bring honor,
for the sake of your loyal love and faithfulness.
2 Why should the nations say,
"Where is their God?"
3 Our God is in heaven.
He does whatever he pleases.
4 Their idols are made of silver and gold—
they are man–made.
5 They have mouths, but cannot speak,
eyes, but cannot see,
6 ears, but cannot hear,
noses, but cannot smell,
7 hands, but cannot touch,
feet, but cannot walk.
They cannot even clear their throats.
8 Those who make them will end up like them,
as will everyone who trusts in them.
9 O Israel, trust in the LORD.
He is their deliverer and protector.
10 O family of Aaron, trust in the LORD.
He is their deliverer and protector.
11 You loyal followers of the LORD, trust in the LORD.
He is their deliverer and protector.
12 The LORD takes notice of us; he will bless—
he will bless the family of Israel,
he will bless the family of Aaron.
13 He will bless his loyal followers,
both young and old.
14 May he increase your numbers,
yours and your children's.

Psalm 115 (continued)

15 May you be blessed by the LORD,
the Creator of heaven and earth.
16 The heavens belong to the LORD,
but the earth he has given to mankind.
17 The dead do not praise the LORD,
nor do any of those who descend
into the silence of death.
18 But we will praise the LORD
now and forevermore.
Praise the LORD!

Psalm 116

1 I love the LORD
because he heard my plea for mercy,
2 and listened to me.
As long as I live, I will call to him when I need help.
3 The ropes of death tightened around me,
the snares of Sheol confronted me.
I was confronted with trouble and sorrow.
4 I called on the name of the LORD,
"Please, LORD, rescue my life!"
5 The LORD is merciful and fair;
our God is compassionate.
6 The LORD protects the untrained;
I was in serious trouble and he delivered me.
7 Rest once more, my soul,
for the LORD has vindicated you.
8 Yes, LORD, you rescued my life from death,
kept my eyes from tears
and my feet from stumbling.
9 I will serve the LORD
in the land of the living.
10 I had faith when I said,

Psalm 116 (continued)

"I am severely oppressed."
11 I rashly declared,
"All men are liars."
12 How can I repay the LORD
for all his acts of kindness to me?
13 I will celebrate my deliverance,
and call on the name of the LORD.
14 I will fulfill my vows to the LORD
before all his people.
15 The LORD values
the lives of his faithful followers.
16 Yes, LORD! I am indeed your servant;
I am your servant, the son of your female servant.
You saved me from death.
17 I will present a thank offering to you,
and call on the name of the LORD.
18 I will fulfill my vows to the LORD
before all his people,
19 in the courts of the LORD's temple,
in your midst, O Jerusalem.
Praise the LORD!

SOAP / *Psalm 116:12*
SCRIPTURE / *Write out the SOAP verses*

_____

_____

_____

_____

_____

_____

_____

_____

_____

_____

_____

_____

_____

_____

_____

_____

_____

OBSERVATION / *Write 3 - 4 observations*

_____

_____

_____

_____

_____

_____

_____

_____

APPLICATION / *Write down 1 - 2 applications*

PRAYER / *Write out a prayer over what you learned*

*Write three things you are thankful for
today and why each one brings you joy.*

ONE

....

....

....

....

....

....

....

TWO

....

....

....

....

....

....

....

THREE

....

....

....

....

....

....

....

READ

Psalm 117

1 Praise the LORD, all you nations.
Applaud him, all you foreigners.
2 For his loyal love towers over us,
and the LORD's faithfulness endures.
Praise the LORD.

Psalm 118

1 Give thanks to the LORD, for he is good,
and his loyal love endures.
2 Let Israel say,
"Yes, his loyal love endures."
3 Let the family of Aaron say,
"Yes, his loyal love endures."
4 Let the loyal followers of the LORD say,
"Yes, his loyal love endures."
5 In my distress I cried out to the LORD.
The LORD answered me and put me in a wide open place.
6 The LORD is on my side; I am not afraid.
What can people do to me?
7 The LORD is on my side as my helper.
I look in triumph on those who hate me.
8 It is better to take shelter in the LORD
than to trust in people.
9 It is better to take shelter in the LORD
than to trust in princes.
10 All the nations surrounded me.
Indeed, in the name of the LORD I pushed them away.
11 They surrounded me, yes, they surrounded me.
Indeed, in the name of the LORD I pushed them away.
12 They surrounded me like bees.
But they disappeared as quickly as a fire among thorns.
Indeed, in the name of the LORD I pushed them away.
13 "You aggressively attacked me and
tried to knock me down,
but the LORD helped me.

Psalm 118 (continued)

14 The Lord gives me strength and protects me;
he has become my deliverer."
15 They celebrate deliverance in the tents of the godly.
The Lord's right hand conquers.
16 The Lord's right hand gives victory;
the Lord's right hand conquers.
17 I will not die, but live,
and I will proclaim what the Lord has done.
18 The Lord severely punished me,
but he did not hand me over to death.
19 Open for me the gates of the just king's temple.
I will enter through them and give thanks to the Lord.
20 This is the Lord's gate—
the godly enter through it.
21 I will give you thanks, for you answered me,
and have become my deliverer.
22 The stone that the builders discarded
has become the cornerstone.
23 This is the Lord's work.
We consider it amazing!
24 This is the day the Lord has brought about.
We will be happy and rejoice in it.
25 Please, Lord, deliver!
Please, Lord, grant us success!
26 May the one who comes in the
name of the Lord be blessed.
We will pronounce blessings on you in the Lord's temple.
27 The Lord is God, and he has delivered us.
Tie the offering with ropes
to the horns of the altar.
28 You are my God, and I will give you thanks.
You are my God and I will praise you.
29 Give thanks to the Lord, for he is good
and his loyal love endures.

It is the
happiness
of heaven
to have
God be all
in all.

Jeremiah Burroughs

SOAP / *Psalm 118:13–14*
SCRIPTURE / *Write out the SOAP verses*

_____

_____

_____

_____

_____

_____

_____

_____

_____

_____

_____

_____

_____

_____

_____

_____

_____

_____

OBSERVATION / *Write 3 - 4 observations*

_____

_____

_____

_____

_____

_____

_____

_____

APPLICATION / *Write down 1 - 2 applications*

PRAYER / *Write out a prayer over what you learned*

THANKFUL
WEEK 2 · THURSDAY

Write three things you are thankful for
today and why each one brings you joy.

ONE

....
....
....
....
....
....
....

TWO

....
....
....
....
....
....
....

THREE

....
....
....
....
....
....
....

WEEK 2
Friday

READ

Psalm 119:1–40

א *(Alef)*

1 How blessed are those whose actions are blameless,
who obey the law of the LORD.
2 How blessed are those who observe his rules,
and seek him with all their heart,
3 who, moreover, do no wrong,
but follow in his footsteps.
4 You demand that your precepts
be carefully kept.
5 If only I were predisposed
to keep your statutes.
6 Then I would not be ashamed,
if I were focused on all your commands.
7 I will give you sincere thanks,
when I learn your just regulations.
8 I will keep your statutes.
Do not completely abandon me.

ב *(Bet)*

9 How can a young person maintain a pure life?
By guarding it according to your instructions.
10 With all my heart I seek you.
Do not allow me to stray from your commands.
11 In my heart I store up your words,
so I might not sin against you.
12 You deserve praise, O LORD.
Teach me your statutes.
13 With my lips I proclaim
all the regulations you have revealed.
14 I rejoice in the lifestyle prescribed by your rules
as if they were riches of all kinds.
15 I will meditate on your precepts
and focus on your behavior.
16 I find delight in your statutes;
I do not forget your instructions.

Psalm 119:1–40 (continued)

ג *(Gimel)*

17 Be kind to your servant.
Then I will live and keep your instructions.
18 Open my eyes so I can truly see
the marvelous things in your law.
19 I am a resident foreigner in this land.
Do not hide your commands from me.
20 I desperately long to know
your regulations at all times.
21 You reprimand arrogant people.
Those who stray from your commands are doomed.
22 Spare me shame and humiliation,
for I observe your rules.
23 Though rulers plot and slander me,
your servant meditates on your statutes.
24 Yes, I find delight in your rules;
they give me guidance.

ד *(Dalet)*

25 I collapse in the dirt.
Revive me with your word.
26 I told you about my ways and you answered me.
Teach me your statutes.
27 Help me to understand what your precepts mean.
Then I can meditate on your marvelous teachings.
28 I collapse from grief.
Sustain me by your word.
29 Remove me from the path of deceit.
Graciously give me your law.
30 I choose the path of faithfulness;
I am committed to your regulations.
31 I hold fast to your rules.
O Lord, do not let me be ashamed.
32 I run along the path of your commands,
for you enable me to do so.

Psalm 119:1–40 (continued)

ה *(He)*

33 Teach me, O Lord, the lifestyle
prescribed by your statutes,
so that I might observe it continually.
34 Give me understanding so that
I might observe your law,
and keep it with all my heart.
35 Guide me in the path of your commands,
for I delight to walk in it.
36 Give me a desire for your rules,
rather than for wealth gained unjustly.
37 Turn my eyes away from what is worthless.
Revive me with your word.
38 Confirm to your servant your promise,
which you made to the one who honors you.
39 Take away the insults that I dread.
Indeed, your regulations are good.
40 Look, I long for your precepts.
Revive me with your deliverance.

SOAP / *Psalm 119:15–16*
SCRIPTURE / *Write out the SOAP verses*

_____

_____

_____

_____

_____

_____

_____

_____

_____

_____

_____

_____

_____

_____

_____

_____

OBSERVATION / *Write 3 - 4 observations*

_____

_____

_____

_____

_____

_____

_____

_____

APPLICATION / *Write down 1 - 2 applications*

PRAYER / *Write out a prayer over what you learned*

*Write three things you are thankful for
today and why each one brings you joy.*

ONE

....

....

....

....

....

....

....

TWO

....

....

....

....

....

....

....

THREE

....

....

....

....

....

....

....

REFLECT

Record an application you learned from your SOAP study this week and how you will practically implement it in your life.

....

....

....

....

....

....

....

....

....

....

....

....

....

....

....

....

....

....

....

....

....

....

....

....

....

....

JOURNAL
your thoughts

....
....
....
....
....
....
....
....
....
....
....
....
....
....
....
....
....
....
....
....
....
....
....
....
....
....

JOURNAL

your thoughts

....
....
....
....
....
....
....
....
....
....
....
....
....
....
....
....
....
....
....
....
....
....
....
....
....

Join Us

ONLINE
lovegodgreatly.com

JOURNALS
lovegodgreatly.com/store

FACEBOOK
lovegodgreatly

INSTAGRAM
@lovegodgreatlyofficial

APP
Love God Greatly

....

CONTACT US
info@lovegodgreatly.com

CONNECT
#LoveGodGreatly

What we offer

35+ Translations
Bible Reading Plans
Online Bible Study
Love God Greatly App
Over 200 Countries Served
Bible Study Journals
Community Groups
Love God Greatly Bible
Love God Greatly Journal

Each study includes

Three Weekly Blog Posts
Daily Devotions
Memory Verses
Weekly Challenges
Weekly Reflection Questions
Bridge Reading Plan

Other studies

The Gospel of Mark
Everlasting Covenant
Jesus Our Everything
Know Love
Empowered: Yesterday and Today
Risen
Draw Near
Beatitudes
Esther
Words Matter
Walking in Victory
To Do Justice, To Love Kindness, To Walk Humbly
Faithful Love
Choose Brave
Savior
Promises of God
Love the Loveless
Truth Over Lies
1 & 2 Thessalonians
Fear & Anxiety
James

His Name Is...
Philippians
1 & 2 Timothy
Sold Out
Ruth
Broken & Redeemed
Walking in Wisdom
God With Us
In Everything Give Thanks
You Are Forgiven
David
Ecclesiastes
Growing Through Prayer
Names of God
Galatians
Psalm 119
1st & 2nd Peter
Made For Community
The Road To Christmas
The Source Of Gratitude
You Are Loved

Printed in Great Britain
by Amazon

25388633R00123